Praise for Michael Reist

"For Reist, one of the most important steps in dealing with boy energy is not to tranquilize, but to empathize. He invites educators to try and place themselves in a 10-year-old boy's shoes, and build their lesson plans from there."

— STEPHEN SCHARPER, THE *TORONTO STAR*

"Michael Reist communicates some essential truths about boys, parenting and being human."

— MICHAEL BELLROSE, *PROFESSIONALLY SPEAKING*

"I found your presentation transformational. I was one of the many in the audience taking notes as fast as I could. It is so important to be able to listen to your experiences from 30 years of working in the public school system. There is so much we can learn from you."

— CANADIAN ASTRONAUT DAVID WILLIAMS

"I think every parent, teacher, coach and grandparent should read this book for its candor and incredibly helpful tips on supporting boys in the best possible way."

— MOTHER OF FIVE BOYS AND ONE GIRL ON
RAISING BOYS IN A NEW KIND OF WORLD

"Thanks for standing up for boys!"

— MOTHER OF TWO BOYS

"Dear mike, (as u say) ure presentation wuz ausome! Im actually the gurl who u gave puddy 2 when u came 2 WOODLANDZ (my grade 7 school) It wuz so tru & i can go up 2 MY MOM & say I LEARNED SOMTHIN 2DAY ! I mean u talked so much stuff into ME! THX SOOO MUCHH!!!"

DE SEVEN

D1516941

What Every Parent Should Know About School

What Every Parent Should Know About School

MICHAEL REIST

DUNDURN
TORONTO

Editor: Jennifer McKnight
Design: Jesse Hooper
Printer: Webcom

Library and Archives Canada Cataloguing in Publication

Reist, Michael, author
    What every parent should know about school / Michael Reist.

Includes bibliographical references and index.
Issued in print and electronic formats.
ISBN 978-1-4597-1904-0 (pbk.).-- ISBN 978-1-4597-1905-7 (pdf).--ISBN 978-1-4597-1906-4 (epub)

    1. School environment--Canada. 2. Classroom environment--Canada. 3. Education--Parent participation. I. Title.

LC210.8.C2R44 2013   371.00971   C2013-902946-X
                                               C2013-902947-8

1   2   3   4   5   17   16   15   14   13

Conseil des Arts du Canada   Canada Council for the Arts   Canada   ONTARIO ARTS COUNCIL CONSEIL DES ARTS DE L'ONTARIO

We acknowledge the support of the **Canada Council for the Arts** and the **Ontario Arts Council** for our publishing program. We also acknowledge the financial support of the **Government of Canada** through the **Canada Book Fund** and **Livres Canada Books**, and the **Government of Ontario** through the **Ontario Book Publishing Tax Credit** and the **Ontario Media Development Corporation**.

Care has been taken to trace the ownership of copyright material used in this book. The author and the publisher welcome any information enabling them to rectify any references or credits in subsequent editions.

J. Kirk Howard, President

Printed and bound in Canada.

Visit us at
Dundurn.com | *Pinterest.com/dundurnpress* | *@dundurnpress* | *Facebook.com/dundurnpress*

Dundurn	Gazelle Book Services Limited	Dundurn
3 Church Street, Suite 500	White Cross Mills	2250 Military Road
Toronto, Ontario, Canada	High Town, Lancaster, England	Tonawanda, NY
M5E 1M2	L41 4XS	U.S.A. 14150

This book is dedicated to every child who hates going to school.
(We're working on it.)

Contents

"I believe that older people who have scarcely anything to lose ought to be willing to speak out on behalf of those who are young and who are subject to much greater restraint."

— ALBERT EINSTEIN

"The test of the morality of a society is what it does for its children."

— DIETRICH BONHOEFFER

"We had one main idea: to make the school fit the child — instead of making the child fit the school."

— A.S. NEILL, FOUNDER OF SUMMERHILL SCHOOL

"To treat everyone the same is to treat them unequally."

— MEL LEVINE

"Grown-ups never understand anything by themselves, and it is tiresome for children to be always and forever explaining things to them."

— ANTOINE DE SAINT-EXUPÉRY

Acknowledgements

I am hugely indebted to the excellent marketing work of Karen McMullin, publicity manager at Dundurn, for her incredible expertise at getting my work out to a wide audience. Thanks also to Allister Thompson, senior editor at Dundurn, for teaching me to look at my writing differently, and to Jennifer McKnight, editor, for her helpful advice and expert editing.

I attended school for twenty years and taught there for thirty. For the past ten years I have worked one-on-one with students of all ages, mostly boys. In all these situations I met children for whom school caused great frustration, anger, and resentment. I am indebted to them for their honesty, sincerity, and suggestions for what needs to change.

I would like to acknowledge my mentors in education, none of whom I have ever met: A.S. Neill, John Holt, Ivan Illich, Neil Postman, Paulo Freire, Maria Montessori, Parker Palmer, and Alice Miller.

My heartfelt love and thanks to my beautiful, intelligent children Thomas, Rachel, Justin, and Luke, who showed me what learning really is, and my wife, Linda, who challenges me to grow every day. This book would not have been possible without her daily love and support.

Who Should Read This Book?

When I address this book to parents, I am including teachers and administrators at all levels of the education system; most of whom are parents too. This is not a book about us and them. It is a book for all of us. We are all products of the system, we all create the system, and we can all change the system. Many parents are not completely satisfied with what schools are, and it is important to say that many teachers and administrators feel the same way. Those who work within the system are reluctant to criticize it because it's all they know. They are too busy to formulate alternatives and, quite simply, it is the hand that feeds them. But, in the end, all parents, all people concerned about the well-being of our children, need to engage in a serious, adult, intelligent, informed, and respectful discussion about what school is and what it *could* be. This book is meant to be an instigator for that discussion.

For many children, school is a great place. They are happy to go every morning and they look back fondly on their past experiences. There are many great schools with wonderful teachers whose classrooms are a joy to be in. Many parents are quite satisfied with the education system as it is. Others acknowledge the need for some changes, but nothing radical. "There's always room for improvement." These anecdotal reports are valid, but I do not think they describe the overall situation in our schools today. In this book, I am not speaking about particular schools, but schools in general. Some readers will see their own experiences or those of their children described in these pages. Others will not. To the extent that these issues exist anywhere, they bear discussion, and I would argue that the issues discussed in this book are relevant to every school in North America.

How to Read This Book

This book is written for the age of the Internet, the screen, and the video game. While it follows something of a logical-linear progression, the sections may be read in any order. Open the book wherever you like, and start reading. That is the new paradigm. We learn by the logical-linear development of a central thesis, but we also learn by random chance and thinking by association, spiralling back to the same ideas again and again. Randomness and repetition are keys to learning.

The Lesson Plan

Objectives:

1. To understand:
   - what goes on inside of schools
   - what it feels like to be in school
   - why kids behave the way they do there
   - why adults behave the way they do there
2. To feel greater empathy for children who go to school.
3. To think of ways school could be improved.
4. To apply this knowledge in particular situations.

Resources Required:
- This book
- Reflection on your own experience of school
- Listening to your children's experience of school
- Imagination
- Creativity
- Courage

Procedure:
- Read this book.
- Note that some ideas will be repeated several times. Repetition is the key to learning. We seldom learn something by hearing it only once.

Evaluation:

- There will be a test at the end of the book.
- It will be evaluated by future generations.

Criteria for Evaluation:

- Happy children who enjoy learning.

1

Let's Open Up School and Look Inside!
THE PHYSICAL ENVIRONMENT OF SCHOOL

Parents stand outside the fortress of school and wonder what goes on in there. In the earliest grades parents are allowed into the classroom and get a glimpse of the early stages of the process. The number of those who take advantage of this opportunity is relatively small. As the child advances through the system, the parent tends to become less and less involved. When you hand your child over to the institution, you lose a lot of control. We come to see this huge loss of parental involvement as normal. "They know what they are doing. It is not my place to comment or ask questions."

So many parents have told me with sadness how their child changed for the worse once they entered school. Why does this have to be the case? Why do we accept this as normal? When our children go to school, they should progress. School should be a place where children thrive and flourish and become even more confident and capable than they were before. School should be a place where social relationships are positive and expand the personality of the child. For many children school is a place where confidence is eroded and one is made to feel incapable, where social relationships degenerate into a competition based on social acceptance and fear of exclusion.

School has become a hermetically sealed world. It is not open to outside scrutiny and certainly not outside criticism. A healthy institution is one that is capable of self-reflection, self-criticism, and self-correction. By this definition school has become a very unhealthy place, not only for the students, but for the adults who work there. There is a danger of concluding that there is some kind of conspiracy on the part of the adults who work in schools. This is not the case at all. The adults who work in our schools are as much victims of the dysfunctional institution as the students are. In one of Steve Jobs's last interviews he said, "What people need to realize is it's all made up — and by people no smarter than you." This is a fundamental principle that we need to embrace in the twenty-first century. Institutions and systems that we see as inevitable do not have to be. They are social constructs that we have all agreed to call normal. School is one of the most normal of all our institutions. We just assume school as a given. School is our most entrenched institution. We are all "schooled" ourselves, so we see it as natural for our kids to be schooled in the same way. We exercise willful blindness to the ways in which it hurt us, stunted us, or inhibited our growth, and we exercise willful blindness to what it does to our children. How many parents have watched a different child come home from school than the one they sent?

Parents need to become more involved in our schools, and schools need to let parents in. Parents need to sit at the table where decisions are being made about curriculum, evaluation, discipline, budgets, and teacher performance. Parents should not run schools, but they should be a more active part of the team that does. Parents would bring a very different perspective to the table, and they would also create a greater degree of accountability. This book is a primer for parents on the inner workings of school, and a call to get involved and make a difference in the most powerful institution affecting our children.

The Great Race Called School

In the early twenty-first century, most of our institutions are being questioned and are teetering under the weight of their own ineffectiveness. People have lost faith in the democratic process and don't trust politicians. People have lost faith in organized religion and don't trust its priests and minsters. Even capitalism, the modern international religion, has come to be questioned, and people have growing contempt for the 1 percent the system favours disproportionately. However, there is still one institution that we seem to cling to — the institution of school. We believe in it as a meritocracy, but we also believe that it is a place where hard work will pay off, where there is some kind of direct correlation between effort and reward. We also believe in school as the great mechanism that will help to determine our place in the social order, primarily the economic order. School has become the great obstacle course that every person must run in order to determine their place in the pecking order of adulthood. Teachers and professors have become the priests of credentialism — a system in which pieces of paper (diplomas and certificates) will grant you passage to the next level in the game. Each level of the game is simply designed as preparation for the next level. Preschool is the preparation ground for elementary school, elementary school is the preparation ground for high school, and high school is the preparation ground for university and college. University and college credentials are the most valuable tickets granting admission to positions within corporate capitalism. The education system serves itself and the economic system. The starter pistol is fired in preschool or kindergarten, and the race is on.

The fallout from such a system is clear: kids who are stressed, kids who lack confidence in themselves, kids who are depressed and addicted, kids who are in conflict with their parents, kids who think they are stupid, and kids who do not know themselves. Institutions become dysfunctional when they continue to function but do not serve their intended purpose. Because school has come to serve other interests, we have lost sight of the true purpose of school. There are many interests which school could be said to legitimately serve, but the two most important are the individual child and the common good. (I use the term common good instead of society because society is a matrix of many interests, including the economic one. Economic interests do not always serve the common good.) School does not always serve the student, nor does it always serve the common good.

Imagine a pyramid. The base represents all of the kids who enter the educational system. The tip represents those who survive the system and come out "on top." This image raises two questions: what happened to all the kids who started out at the bottom and didn't make it to subsequent levels of the pyramid? And secondly, what kinds of people did the pyramid produce, including both the people that the pyramid worked for and the ones that it didn't?

The School Race and the Rat Race

Free-market capitalism is based on competition. It could be argued that this system is responsible for most of the innovation and the rise in standard of living since the Industrial Revolution. The list of products and services we enjoy today is a very long one, and much of the credit lies with free-market capitalism. Jungian psychology suggests that everything has a shadow side, a side we are not so willing to look at because it does not fit the official version, what Jungians call the persona or mask. While capitalism has accomplished great things, it has created a very competitive culture where the most aggressive person ends up on top, where might makes right and the world is divided into winners and losers.

Movies like *Citizen Kane* and Arthur Miller's play, *Death of a Salesman* have tried to portray this darker side of capitalism. For all his wealth, all Kane was ever seeking was Rosebud, the emblem of a happy childhood from which he was prematurely torn. Willy Loman spends his entire life chasing the American Dream only to end up a pathetic old man trying to kill himself with a rubber tube attached to the pilot light of the furnace. For every Donald Trump there are countless men and women for whom the system did not work. When the credit crisis of 2008 hit, the latent anger about capitalism erupted in the form of the Occupy Wall Street movement. Their slogan, "We are the 99 Percent," represented a huge challenge to the central claim of capitalism that anyone can be a millionaire. All you have to do is work hard. For many hard-working people, this was simply not true, and there was a perception that the 1 percent, the millionaires and billionaires, were not working that hard to get what they had.

Students feel a great sense of fear about the future because they are intimidated by the system that they feel will determine that future. This is where school meets capitalism. School has become the sorting room for the social order, and capitalism relies on schools to filter out the weak and promote the strong. School is no longer a preparation for entry into the workplace. It is more like a testing-ground, a gladiatorial arena where those who survive move on. Like *The Hunger Games*, life for many young people feels like a fight to the death, where the cruelest, least-empathetic person will win.

When we talk about "disengaged youth," we are talking about those students who do not see any hope for themselves in this competitive system.

There seem to be fewer and fewer places at the top, or even in the middle. At least in video games they can rise to the top through their efforts. At least in video games they can get some sense of validation and success.

School Is Our Second Home

Next to the family, school is by far our most powerful and influential social institution. Almost every person will have intimate contact with school over a long period of time and during one's most impressionable years. So much of what we become as individuals and, therefore, as a society, is shaped by our experiences at school. There is no more important place to look if we want to talk about social change and the maximizing of individual potential. Of all our remaining institutions, school has the potential to change the world the most. We need people who are strong, confident, and creative. We need people who will take on the difficult social tasks that lie before us: the environment, poverty, social injustice, racism, war. It could be argued that many of the social issues we face have, in fact, been created by our educational system. If school is the cause of our problems, it could also be the solution to our problems.

The Glass Wall between Parents and School

Parents do not make up a significant part of the power structure of the school. When parents interact with schools, there can be a glass wall — an invisible barrier between the parent on one side and teachers and administrators on the other. The parent feels they are helplessly looking in on a world they have put their child into, but over which they have little control. If we were to draw the governance structure of school, it would look something like this:

Voting Citizens (first tier of elected representation by parents)
Elected Government
Ministry or Department of Education
Boards of Education or School Districts
Elected Trustees (second tier of elected representation by parents)
Superintendents

Principals
Teachers
Children

According to this governance model, parental involvement would seem to be restricted to the election of surrogates who will make key decisions. In some jurisdictions we see parental advisory councils at the ministry or board level or parent councils at the school level, but their power is quite limited. In terms of accountability and transparency, parents are not really part of the day-to-day running of schools, nor are they really part of any larger process. Parents feel as though they are onlookers. Some parents are very comfortable handing their children over to the institution and have an abiding trust in its good judgement. For others, there is disillusionment ranging from vague concern to outright distrust or even alarm.

A fundamental question then arises. What recourse does a parent have when they have serious and intelligent concerns about the system itself or about the way their child is experiencing the system?

There are very few points of entry for parents right now. On a day-to-day basis, phone calls or face-to-face meetings with the teacher, principal, or superintendent are the standard mode of input into what happens at school. On a broader level, there is the parent council, which in most jurisdictions has devolved into a fundraising committee. There is little discussion of school policy, pedagogy, hiring, or budgetary spending. Theoretically, a parent's input happens through their elected school board trustees who make more substantive decisions, but, in a large school board, these decisions are being made for many schools over a large geographic area for thousands of students.

Schools Need Parents

In the school of the future, parents will be much more involved in the day-to-day running of the school and in many of the decisions that make up its culture and tone. In the nineteenth-century, before the creation of factory schools, it was common for each school to have its own board of trustees, made up almost entirely of parents of children who attended that particular school. This is still the case with smaller private schools.

Teachers were accountable directly to parents. Today teachers see themselves as accountable to their principal or their school board. The parent is a distant figure to be fended off or placated when they do come calling — usually for negative reasons.

The educational bureaucracy is not the only force that has created this state of affairs. Parents themselves tend to hand their children over to the institution and surrender (willingly or unwillingly) much control over the direction of their child's life. If we were to create a school system that allowed for more parental involvement, it would require extra effort from parents to educate themselves about the issues facing teachers and administrators in a school. Greater parental involvement should not take the form of another tier of governance hanging over a teacher's head. It should take the form of a dialogue where the parent stands to learn as much as the teacher, and where the parent may be required to change his or her expectations about what school can and cannot do.

But what about the fact that many parents have vastly differing visions of what school should be? This is where intentional communities become important.

A Common Vision: Intentional Communities

One of the solutions to the negative influences of mass institutional life would be the re-configuration of schools as intentional communities. An intentional community is one in which there is a common underlying ethos as to why the community exists, what its values are, and what it wants to accomplish. Once these foundations exist, *how* to accomplish these goals will emerge naturally. We see this phenomenon in small private schools organized around a core vision. It is hard to create a sense of community in a large school that is part of a large school district. Schools become franchises or branch plants of a board of education that might even be located in another city. In modern factory schools, particularly in larger urban areas, there is often little sense of community. Students are bussed in from distant places, and teachers commute in from other towns. There is no common denominator or shared vision.

Intentional communities can give their members a sense of identity and belonging that strengthens the self. We are social beings who seek group identities and allegiances. Testimony to our need for smaller group-ings on a human scale is the organic formation of tribes and groups even within large factory schools. One will find the drama kids, the band nerds, the jocks, and the computer geeks coalescing within schools. Many kids are able to survive the alienating effects of large institutions because of the support, sense of identity, and camaraderie they derive from these groups. In the past, these groups may have been labelled "cliques" by the dominant group who were frustrated by their unwillingness to become absorbed into the grey mass. Sub-groups in a school always stand as a challenge to the homogenizing influence of the institution. They play an extremely vital role in the ecosystem.

Nature abhors a monoculture. Biodiversity should be encouraged within large factory schools and within large school districts. We know about magnet schools or focus schools, but there are also focus or magnet classrooms and hallways where students with particular interests can go to feel safe, validated, and stimulated in their area of interest. This is key to the mental health, not to mention the academic success, of students.

Sometimes teachers and administrators pull in very different direc-tions. Teachers within a school may have a broad range of educational phil-osophies and methods, often at odds with each other. For some children, going from class to class can be quite a confusing experience, as they find themselves faced with a number of different classroom management styles, value systems, and core philosophies of education. They must constantly accommodate themselves to the adult at the front of the classroom.

Open enrollment policies, school vouchers, tuition tax credits, charter schools, and magnet or focus schools are among the options that have been rapidly growing in popularity over the past few decades. All of these options provide a positive alternative to the factory, branch-plant model of public education because they provide a greater possibility for the formation of intentional communities.

There are two main criticisms of school choice and smaller schools. One is that choice tends to favour upper- and middle-class parents who are more equipped to make these choices and have the means to follow through on the practical implications (like transportation). The second criticism is that small intentional communities can become closed off, cultish bubbles antagonistic to the common good.

Intentional communities would require us to take greater responsibility for what schools are. George Bernard Shaw said, "Liberty means responsibility. That is why most men dread it." We either do not want to take responsibility ourselves or we do not trust others to exercise it properly. One of the slogans of the Party in George Orwell's *1984* was "Freedom is slavery." Freedom implies slavery to choice and choice implies taking responsibility for the choices you make. Another slogan of the party was "Obedience is strength." In other words, obedience is easier than freedom. Doing what you're told is easier than deciding what you should do. This is the dark side of the monolithic public education system where one size fits all.

There is a not-so-subtle subtext in public education that the status quo is best, the state knows better, uniformity and obedience are good things, and diversity is just too hard to monitor and control — anything could happen! Teachers' unions join in this argument largely out of self-interest. A uniform monolithic system requires a priestly caste that is pure and orthodox. The concern is that if the school system is fragmented, all sorts of people could end up teaching our children. Whatever the problems are that would arise from greater diversity, these problems can be dealt with. The possibility of problems that might come with change is no reason to obey the status quo blindly.

Schools Need to Listen to the Voices of Children

When we talk about intentional communities, there is a danger that we will only be talking about the intentions of parents — that children are objects to be acted upon and should have no say in the kinds of environments in which they are to spend a large part of their lives. Children of all ages need to be listened to and taken seriously. If we want to apply a consumer model to school, it could be argued that students are the consumers, not parents. When we take our family to a restaurant, we ask our children what they would like to eat. When we put our kids in school, they are served a dish they have not chosen.

There is no customer satisfaction questionnaire at school. Many businesses have a box by the door with a sign above it saying "Tell us how we did." There are even forms you can fill out to help you organize your thoughts. There is no such form for kids in school. There should be.

With so many of our decisions concerning our children, we tell ourselves we know best, that we have their best interests at heart, that they are too young to decide for themselves, that even if they don't like it, it's for their own good. These attitudes can blind us to our children's true needs. They serve to reinforce our own pre-conceived notions. If we were to listen honestly to what our children are saying — especially about school — we would be forced to change, and that is the crux of the problem in education: fear of change.

The Factory School

Before we can change schools, we need to see their mechanical structure. And we need to see this structure as arbitrary and, therefore, changeable. The mechanisms of school are not set in stone. We have designed school on the model of the factory. Students are products that we produce by applying one process to all of them. We take the raw material of the young child and we turn it into something of value. We have great faith in this process, and we can hardly imagine another paradigm. Since the Industrial Revolution, we have come to place great faith in scientific, technological, and mechanistic processes. We like their uniformity, predictability, and efficiency. The time has come to question the paradigm of the factory. If you can judge the factory by its products, then the system is not as efficient as we thought. School reminds me of those old Soviet factories that were designed to give jobs to as many people as possible, not for productivity. The Soviet state created a bloated bureaucracy because it was based on an ideology of the rule of the working class, an illusion like ours that schools serve the best interests of kids. Schools serve themselves at least as much as they serve the child.

Schools do not serve the needs of the *whole* child. In order to serve the whole child, a complex organic being, we would need to adopt an organic metaphor or paradigm. Let's not talk about judging the factory by its products. Let's talk about judging the tree by its fruits. Germany gave us the word "kindergarten," or "child garden," and we use that label for the first year or two of the process. But then in grade one things get serious and it's time to put away all that play and get on with the program. What if the decentered, child-centred approach of kindergarten were to be carried forward? Student apathy and disengagement increases in direct proportion to the increase in the mechanistic approach taken. Kids begin to realize that they are objects being acted upon. They are not the actors. They are told to take responsibility for their own learning, but they are never really given responsibility for it. The adults around them see it as their responsibility to teach the child, to do something to the child. The child is not the agent of his own learning. The adults are in control, and the child is nothing but the passive recipient of what the adults want to do to them.

The Decentered School

The school of the future will be a decentered school. We once talked about the child-centred school, but the problem with that model was that we fell into a single definition of what a child was and returned to the mechanistic approach of meeting the needs of that generic child. The decentered school might even be called the fragmented school. In the future, we will no longer be able to talk about school as a single entity. School will not be one thing; it will be many different kinds of things. The idea of being a student will evolve beyond our current recognition. The boundary between school and life will become more blurred.

This will be a huge challenge to the credential-granting function of our institutions. We live under the illusion right now that a high school diploma means one thing, that it is a kind of standardized certification, that a high school graduate has a certain knowledge base and skill set that can be proven by the existence of the piece of paper. Anyone close to the educational system knows that this is not true. Since the end of the Second World War schools have taken in such huge numbers of children that they have had no choice but to modify curriculum standards to be able to process as many of these children as possible. In the 1950s and 60s, there was some attempt to hold a standardized yardstick in place, and kids failed or dropped out in significant numbers. By the 1970s and 80s social promotion crept into elementary schools and students were simply pushed along the conveyor belt even though they hadn't met all the specifications of the factory. By the 1980s special education became a huge side industry that created various sub-categories and alternative ways of streaming students who could not meet the standard. All students are now promoted to grade nine and come into a multi-tiered high school system where they move through the grades at various "levels." Social promotion is now creeping into high schools. There is great pressure to move students along whether or not they have met the stated standard. Post-secondary institutions have had to create myriad remedial programs to help students cope with the demands of college and university.

There are two responses to this reality. The first is to go back and try to raise all those dropped bars, to get "back to basics." This is not going to happen. It would require a draconian approach that no one would tolerate, and we are no longer sure what "the basics" are. The other response is to admit that we are living in a new kind of world, and we need a new kind of school system. The factory model no longer works. The subjects refuse to respond to our processes. We need to dismantle the old Soviet-era factories and create a free-market.

In the great Canadian classic novel *Agaguk*, the main character, an Inuit hunter, walks for three days to trade his hard-gotten furs for some much-needed supplies. The Hudson's Bay agent offers him half what the furs are worth, and both men know it. When Agaguk questions the agent's fairness, he is told to take it or leave it and if he causes any more fuss, there will be no future market for his furs. Agaguk is filled with rage and a feeling of impotence. The scene demonstrates very powerfully the problem with monopolies. The Hudson's Bay Company had a monopoly over the fur trade. It could do whatever it wanted, was accountable to no one, and traders had no recourse to a higher authority.

The public school system is also a monopoly. Unless one has the means to pay for private schooling, there is nowhere else to go. The publicly funded school system has no publicly funded competition. If you don't like what's being offered there, you have no alternative. The school system of the future must offer more choice, more variety, and more alternatives. Alternative education programs are currently offered by only some school boards and only cater to a small clientele of "at risk" students. These programs need to expand and morph into a complex array of choices that will eventually replace the core prescribed curriculum.

In the school of the future students will be able to specialize in their areas of strength much sooner. They will be more willing to commit to a process that develops their strengths instead of constantly reminding them of their weaknesses. The notion of a prescribed core curriculum will be transformed into a more organic and less systematized collection of options. It will rely much less on the school building as its locus. Students of the future will be at home, the workplace, or perhaps at school. If they are at school, they might be in a traditional classroom listening to a teacher, but they will just as likely be in the computer lab, the science lab, the visual arts studio, the drama room, the music room, the library, group discussion rooms, or individual cubicles working on a wide variety of individual or group projects. The school building will not be the centre of education. Socrates' academy happened in the market square. It was called the *peripatetic* school — the school of walking around.

In education, one size does not fit all. We have entered into a period of radical democracy in which people demand a voice in how their lives are arranged; they want more control over the way their daily lives are lived. The monolithic, hierarchical, authoritarian school system cannot survive in the age of the smart phone, the Internet, and the video game. We have entered an age of decentered systems. The metaphor of the network has replaced the metaphor of the ladder or the pyramid. In the future, we will continue to "move up," but we will also move across and around and down. Hierarchies and competition may be hard-wired into human nature, but the school of the future will abandon climbing the ladder or winning the race as its central metaphor.

School as a Shopping Mall

We are strongly influenced by the environments in which we live. They reflect who we are, and they create who we are. We must ask ourselves very honestly what our school buildings tell us about ourselves and how they influence us. Schools from the twentieth century were designed largely on the factory or prison model. These were the only institutions we knew of that were designed to deal with large numbers of people, so it was natural that we would copy them. Schools built in the twenty-first century sometimes take on more of the characteristics of a shopping mall. Grand central foyers or hallways have become common with various specialty rooms like the library, the guidance office, etc. lined up like store fronts opening onto a central traffic area. In the factory model, the student is a product and the teachers are the workers. In the prison model, the student is the prisoner and the teachers are the wardens. In the shopping mall, the students are the customers, the teachers are the sales clerks, and learning is the merchandise. The interesting thing about the shopping mall metaphor is that the student can *choose* whether to buy something or not, the teacher has to *sell* the product, and the merchandise being sold has to be made more and more *attractive* to the buyer. The shopping mall model does not bode well for education.

The Wizard of Oz

Another telling detail about the layout of our schools is the placement of the principal's office. In most schools, the main office is a warren of mysterious rooms connected by mysterious hallways and interconnecting doors that almost seem to resemble escape routes for the adults who work there. One is met in the front office by the head secretary, whom many in education jokingly refer to as the most powerful person in the school. She is the gate keeper. She controls much of the flow of information as well as access to teachers and administrators. One must give reasons for wanting to speak and arrange times that are convenient for administrators. For legitimate security reasons, visitors to schools are funnelled immediately to the main office, but once there, the secretaries become something like one of the munchkin guards at the door to Oz deciding whether or not to let Dorothy and her companions in. The other barrier faced by parents is voice mail systems, which have become the impersonal automated gatekeepers for all large institutions.

In the school of the future, administrators will be far more accessible and engaged with students, parents, and teachers. It is not uncommon to see administrators who spend most of the day at a laptop managing the school from a screen or who are simply absent while attending various meetings. The principal as branch manager or the CEO will have to adopt Lee Iacocca's famous model of "management by walking around."

There Is No Such Thing as Nature

Nothing says more about our current school system than the state of its playgrounds. These broad expanses of asphalt and grass are wastelands that teach kids a very negative lesson about the natural world: it doesn't matter; in fact, it doesn't even exist. The natural world is something you see on a screen. There is no such thing as nature in the real world. What incredible potential there is in these blank slates we call playgrounds. Trees, flower gardens, fountains and pools, animals, vegetable gardens, sandboxes — why are these ideas so radical, so unheard of?

In *Last Child in the Woods*, Richard Louv talks about "nature deficit disorder." So many of the problems we see in kids today — anxiety, attention span, behaviour, social skills, cognitive functioning — can be traced back to our lack of connection with nature. For millennia, humans have evolved in close proximity to nature. Our alienation from nature began with the Industrial Revolution, but has reached an unprecedented level today. For many kids, the natural world is something they only see on screens or through a car window. They rarely have physical contact with it. Climbing a tree, putting your feet in water, holding animals and insects — these are things of the past. Nature now is something that makes your clothes dirty or is dangerous.

We have to find ways to bring nature back into children's lives. The playground would be an excellent place to start. What about aquariums and terrariums in the classroom? What about more field trips to natural settings as simple as conservation areas close by the school? And this exposure to nature should be as unstructured and unmediated as possible. A child can't make a daisy chain or catch a frog when they have a pencil and a worksheet in their hands.

2

How Does It Feel to Be at School?

THE EMOTIONAL ENVIRONMENT OF SCHOOL

A child is completely foreign to this organized society of adults. His 'kingdom' is certainly 'not of this world.' He is a stranger to that artificial world which men have built above nature. A child comes into the world as an asocial being since he cannot adapt himself to society nor contribute to its productivity nor influence its structure. He is rather a disturber of the accepted order. A child is asocial in that he is a source of disturbance wherever there are adults, even in his own home. His lack of adaptation to an adult environment is aggravated by the fact that he is naturally active and constitutionally incapable of renouncing this activity.
— Maria Montessori, *The Secret of Childhood*

The Fraser Institute, a conservative Canadian think tank, uses the phrase, "If it matters, measure it." We like to be able to measure things, and we like to hand out pieces of paper that testify to the measurement in the form of report cards, transcripts, diplomas, and certificates. On the other hand, we also believe Antoine de Saint-Exupéry's famous line from *The Little Prince*, "It is only with the heart that one can see rightly; what is essential is invisible to the eye." We have a hard time living by this abstract truth. The percentage grade on a report card carries far more weight than any emotional considerations. Numbers are more important than feelings. And yet feelings are an essential component of learning.

One of the most powerful indications we have that schools need to change is the way children *feel* about school. There are too many children who hate it. As parents, why would we send our children into an environment every day that they hate? As teachers, why would we choose a profession in which our job is to preside over people who find the situation hateful? Why do children cheer when the school busses are cancelled? Kids count down the days to holidays; parents count down the days until holidays are over. What do these behaviours tell us? We accept as normal the idea that school is a place children would choose to avoid if they could, and yet we've also said that it is their second home!

Freedom, Control, Stress, and Happiness: They Are All Connected

We learn better when we are happy and relaxed. When we are stressed and anxious we do not learn as well. The body fills with cortisol, and our brain simply does not function at its optimal level. Stress is related to feelings of powerlessness; the less in control we feel, the more stress we feel. Kids are happy about the snow day because they can now decide what to do with their day. They are free. One of the most powerful lessons we can learn from the democratic free school movement is the value of freedom in the lives of children. When people are free to decide what they will do, when they will do it, and how they will do it, they are much more relaxed. Stress results from being constrained by external forces over which you feel you have no control.

The school of the future is going to have to allow more freedom of choice for students. Freedom teaches responsibility. When we are free to make our own choices, we become responsible for the outcomes. When someone is telling us what to do, we are not required to be responsible. We are only required to be obedient. Traditional factory schooling teaches obedience, it does not teach responsibility.

The Top-Down School

When we raise the topic of freedom and responsibility versus obedience, we have, by extension, raised the issue of power and control. The fundamental question facing us in schools is who is going to have the power and control? Right now, all of the power and control is held by the adults who run the institution, with the most power and control being concentrated at the top of the pyramid in the highest levels of administration. This is where the most important choices are made: What will be taught? How will it be taught? How will the money be spent? Who will be the key players in the game? Which interests will be listened to? Which interests will be ignored? The education system is one of the most top-down institutions we have.

Teachers respond to this top-down system in four ways:

1. UNQUESTIONING SERVANTS
Many teachers are simply unquestioning servants of the system who see their job as simply one of implementing the demands of those higher up the pyramid. These teachers are rewarded by the system and those who will "move up" in the system and perpetuate its modes of functioning are taken from their ranks. These teachers are generally enthusiastic cheerleaders of the system who believe very strongly in what it does and how it does it. They believe in the system with a simple, unquestioning faith. They cannot imagine any alternative, so why doubt the desirability of the status quo?

2. APATHETIC SERVANTS
The second response is resignation or apathy, teachers who go through the motions, feel powerless to change anything, and simply accept the status quo as a given. They do not enthusiastically endorse the system, nor do they criticize it. It is what it is. They have a vague sense of the problems, but no ideas about solutions.

3. ISLAND DWELLERS
The third response is to bracket off the classroom as a place of creative experiment and possible change. While one may feel powerless in the face of the system, the classroom can become an arena in which the core issues in education can be addressed and even remedied. These are the teachers we remember, the creative teachers who were passionate about their subject area, where learning came before all else. Teachers who made personal contact with their students, who formed relationships that were meaningful and respectful. These classrooms are "islands of humanity." They offer hope and feed the souls of those students lucky enough to end

up in them. Students and parents cannot choose these teachers, it is serendipity that will decide which students get them. These island dwellers tolerate the larger system, but do not spend a lot of time or energy serving it. They focus more on their students and their own pedagogy.

4. THOSE WHO LEAVE

The fourth response of teachers to the top-down system is to leave. This is a very disturbing trend. Many promising young teachers have a real vision of what school could be, but when they enter the profession, this vision is not encouraged or developed. In fact, the opposite occurs; they are quickly indoctrinated into the rituals and dogmas of the institution where any kind of questioning is explicitly discouraged. Innovation must take the form of officially approved methods of innovation. The institution always has some current board or ministry initiative that is *de rigueur* for the proselyte who wishes to make a good impression. Some young teachers chafe under this externally imposed "creativity." They are also surprised by the level of apathy or outright subversive behaviour of the students. They expected a happy and co-operative audience, and wonder at the cause of this hostility toward their own good intentions.

Students Living at the Bottom of a Top-Down World

Students are at the very bottom of this top-down system. While teachers have some degree of control over the daily workings of their lives, students have almost none. They respond to the system in the same four ways: unquestioning obedience, apathy, subversive behaviour, and opting out.

1. THE GOOD STUDENT

Some students enjoy the game of school. It suits their personality and temperament. They are more than willing to play along, and they reap the rewards school has to offer: good marks, praise, and, yes, learning. These students will often become teachers.

2. THE BORED STUDENT

Other students, who do not feel comfortable in school or find it boring, become apathetic. They just stop caring — about marks, about learning, about pleasing the teacher. They go through the motions, doing the minimum required. They are not hostile to the system, nor are they engaged in it. It's just something you have to do.

3. THE BAD STUDENT

The third group has either more energy or more passion. They are consciously hostile to the processes of school and seek to subvert the power and authority of the teacher. Sometimes this is based on principle. "You're not the boss of me." "I am the master of my own destiny." Sometimes it is simply a response to sheer boredom. "I am bored to tears with what is going on here, so I'm going to stir things up and get something going." "I'm not getting any positive attention from the system, so I'll try for some negative attention." At least it's attention, and at least it's stimulating.

4. THE DROP-OUT

These might be students who just do not have the cognitive skills that school rewards most — the ability to read and write and do math beyond a functional level — or they might be among the brightest and school is just too boring. They are often students with emotional issues, attention-control issues, or impulse-control issues, which only bring them approbation and isolation in the school setting. On an existential level, these are often the students with the most integrity. They are just not willing to play a game that they feel violates their soul. They are not willing to serve a system in which they do not believe.

Alternatives to Top-Down

In the decentered school, the power will not be concentrated at the top of the pyramid — the ministry, the school board, the principal, the teacher. The power will be concentrated in the learner. The learner will have much more choice about when, where, and how to do things. Learning might happen online, at home, at work — places where the traditional authority figure has no jurisdiction. It will be up to the learner to make it work.

School Is Not a Job

Of course, in the work place there will still be the traditional boss, but that is the nature of the market and part of the student's learning. If one is going to be successful in the workplace as an employee, one will need to adhere to the demands of the employer. This is a reasonable expectation of the workplace. Sometimes educators describe school as parallel to the workplace. You have to be at your job on time, so you have to be in class on time. Your boss won't tolerate laziness, so the teacher won't tolerate laziness. Sometimes we try to present school as a practice ground for the world of work as a way of gaining compliance. It is an outdated approach to school. School is not the workplace, nor should it be. We do not need to model school on other institutions. It is a unique entity that must redesign its power structure so that motivation to learn comes from within the student.

School in Cyberspace

When a student is given the freedom to choose his or her own activities and approaches, the responsibility for completing them lies directly with the student. Students have taken online courses with the assumption that it would be much easier than sitting and listening to a teacher in a regular classroom, only to find that the online course required much more initiative. In the classroom, the locus of control very easily reverts to the teacher, who quickly falls into the role of circus ringmaster. Using rewards and punishments, it is the job of the ringmaster teacher to get students to jump through the various hoops held up. When you take away the ringmaster, the focus returns to its proper place, the student and his or her learning.

The traditional model of the teacher at the front of the classroom will need to come to an end. Students are ready to take ownership for their learning because this is the paradigm they are most familiar with in cyberspace. When you are at a screen, the only way it can work is if you make it work. Cyberspace cannot control you; you control it. Yes, certain screen content can be very seductive and appear to control its audience, but the viewer always has the power to leave. The previous technology environment of television was very passive. Changing the channel was the extent of one's control. In cyberspace the participant is not just a viewer but an active player. This represents a golden opportunity for schooling:

to change the format from the top-down cinder block box to the radically democratic world of cyberspace. It is important to note that this brave new world will only be achieved if cyberspace, particularly the Internet, remains radically democratic. To the extent that corporate interests control the Internet, the freedom of the individual user will be curtailed and experiences had online will become as artificial as those in school.

Authentic learning originates from its truest source: curiosity. If the curiosity of the child could be harnessed at an early age, the process of learning would take care of itself. School is based on the assumption of a reluctant learner, someone who has to be coerced and "motivated" to learn as though it was foreign to the child's nature. What a tragedy! People become what they are perceived to be, and if children are seen to be averse to learning, they will become averse to learning — and the entertainment industry stands ready to fill the void. Through the processes of school, we teach that learning is onerous and foreign to our essential nature and so we rob children of the joy of learning. Think of the four-year-old who is full of questions. Why this? Why that? What is this? What is that? The child is a sponge. School takes this curiosity and shifts the focus from the learner to the teacher. It is not a place of *learning* but a place of *teaching*. The activities of the teacher become the focus instead of those of the child, and the agenda of the teacher becomes more important than the agenda of the child.

Too Many Words, Not Enough Moving Around

Cyberspace has something to teach us about the deficiencies of the cinder block box that is school and the direction change might take. We are living more and more in a visual-spatial world. This is the water in which our children swim. When they come to school, they enter a very different world that is predominantly logical, linear, and verbal. School is a place dominated by reading, writing, speaking, and listening. The child who can master these skills will have a much better chance of success in school. One of the reasons we have seen boys falling behind in school is the fact that the male brain generally favours spatial activities while the female brain is more comfortable with logical-linear-verbal functioning. Boys love cyberspace because it fits their brains better. When boys come into school, they

43

feel a vague (or sometimes not so vague) sense of discomfort. They feel that somehow they don't fit in. They feel that they're not very good at what school is asking them to do. This leads to deeper destructive conclusions like "I'm not very smart," "I'm not very good," and more generally, "girls are smart, boys are stupid." This kind of negative thinking increases as primary grades emphasize literacy more and more. As we are all losing print literacy, we try to push it on our youngest children in the hope of reversing a societal trend. The thought is that if we just start kids earlier on reading and writing, everyone will become more literate. When I look at some of the emails I get from adults or ask about their reading habits, it makes me wonder why we don't have more literacy programs for the adult population. We often place on children our own fears and desires. In this case, the fear is that we ourselves are becoming illiterate and we desire to be able to function better in the realm of words. We should encourage literacy in boys, but we must also find ways of tapping into their natural love of movement.

Sports

Spatial activity should be valued more at school. Math is a spatial activity, and that is one area that is valued. It is also an area where, statistically, boys do quite well. The other spatial activity that we find at school is sports. Let us consider sports as part of a larger continuum of physical activity that starts with unstructured play, moves along to games, and ends with highly structured competitive sports. School has come to emphasize highly structured competitive sports, particularly in middle school and high school. The best athletes are rewarded for their bodily/kinesthetic and spatial prowess, but these make up a very small percentage of students. They are valued and rewarded because of their competitive accomplishments and the pride these bring to the school. There should be a similar emphasis on what are sometimes called "house league" sports. In house league sports the emphasis is on including as many players as possible. Teams are formed from a much larger group and compete among themselves. The most elite private schools incorporate this kind of sport as a matter of course. Public schools have let this kind of activity go. House league sports should be one of the choices available to students as part of normal school life.

Play

At the other end of the spectrum is unstructured play. Again, in our obsession with literacy, we seem to have forgotten the importance of unstructured play. It is seen as a frivolous waste of time largely because the benefits cannot be readily measured. Going back to the Fraser Institute's dictum, "If it matters, measure it," play is a hard thing to measure. And yet we know that the foundations of cognitive functioning and social functioning can be found in play. These are our first and most fundamental attempts to make sense of the world and to learn about ourselves and others. The benefits of play have been well documented, and yet we are suspicious of it. We need to honour unstructured play and, later, structured play more in our schools, especially among the youngest. Every child must get his or her fill of play or the deficit will persist throughout life. One of the reasons we see so many adults who are stuck in a kind of eternal adolescence and are unable to fully assume the responsibilities of adult life is that they did not get enough play in childhood and they spend the rest of their lives trying to fill this unmet need. Adult play has become a huge industry. Children's play has been replaced by programs.

There is much research to show that physical movement of any kind is stimulating to the brain. As *Homo sapiens*, we spent millennia walking, moving our bodies, and manipulating things with our hands. It is only in the last era of human history that we have spent so much time sitting down. It is simply not our natural state, and yet in school we seem to assume that it is natural for a child to sit for long periods of time. A child wiggling and squirming as he builds with his Lego blocks at home is a perfectly natural sight. A child wiggling and squirming in the grade one classroom becomes a child with a problem. Same child, same behaviour, but the setting changes our perception and judgement of the child. We can talk about "appropriate" behaviour, but we must also be willing to temper that judgement with what we know to be "natural" behaviour.

Sensory Processing

The issue of movement has become more important than ever before because of all the time kids spend in front of screens. The current generation is probably the most sedentary in human history. Our streets, parks, and yards are empty. Our kids are sitting at screens. And when they go to school, they are required to sit even more. Children need to get up and move. According to the theory of sensory processing, also called sensory integration, there are eight senses, not just five. In addition to taste, touch, sight, hearing, and smell, we have three other senses: the proprioceptive sense, the vestibular sense, and the interoceptive sense.

The proprioceptive sense is our sense of our muscles and joints and their movement. It is exercised by activities like pushing and pulling. Our vestibular sense is our sense of balance, of the relationship between our inner ear and the surface of the earth. It is exercised in activities such as somersaults or jumping on a trampoline. The interoceptive sense is our sense of our internal organs — knowing one's bladder is full or that one's head aches.

As we move through the developmental stages, these senses must develop independently and in synchronization with all the other eight senses. Some children experience delays in the development of some of these senses or a lack of integration of the messages these senses are sending. Some children are hyper-sensitive in some of these areas, others are hypo-sensitive. What is important is the exercising of these senses in order to achieve integration and equilibrium in their functioning. Many kids today, especially those who spend a lot of time in front of screens and sitting at desks in school, do not get enough sensory stimulation (sensory processing) and therefore do not get a chance to practice sensory integration. They have a poor "sensory diet."

In *The Out-of-Sync Child*, Carol Stock Kranowitz quotes Dr. A. Jean Ayres, the originator of the term sensory integration: "Sensations that make a child happy tend to be integrating." Children know what they need, or, more accurately, children's bodies know what they need. Some kids need to squirm and wiggle. Some kids need to skip and spin down the hall instead of walk. Some kids need to put their head between their legs and see the world upside down. They are not only exercising their bodies, they are exercising their senses. We need to be aware of this need, we need to honour it, and, most of all, we need to allow it — however disruptive to institutional decorum it may be.

3

What Are the Other People at School Like?

THE SOCIAL ENVIRONMENT OF SCHOOL

One of the reasons we send our kids to school is to become socialized. What do we mean by socialization and what are they being socialized into? Socialization should mean learning to function in a variety of social groups, to be able to cope with situations as they arise, and to be able to form meaningful and nurturing relationships with fellow human beings. In school, socialization comes to mean conforming to social norms, whether those social norms are healthy or not. When we enter an institutional setting, is this the same thing as entering society? Institutions have their specific codes of behaviour, which are not always those of society at large. In school one cannot stand up and walk around without asking permission, one has to raise one's hand to speak, and one cannot run or raise one's voice. These are not rules one finds in society at large. We must be aware that when we send our children to an institutional setting for fourteen years, we are not sending them into a natural social setting. It is a very artificial one that some kids will find fits comfortably enough but others will find very uncomfortable. The problem lies in blaming the child who feels uncomfortable in school for his lack of comfort as though there is something wrong with him. Children have no choice about entering this artificial social situation. If we present it to them as natural or normal, they become confused. They have had experiences in the social world of home, extended family, friends, and the marketplace, and they have had experiences of the natural world at the park, camping, hiking, and in the garden. But the environment they find at school is not like either of these.

Learning to Love Big Brother

When I entered school in grade one I remember asking my brother if it was really true that you had to raise your hand to ask a question. When he said it was, I found this very intriguing and wondered what other kinds of secret signs and rituals I would find there. Having spent almost fifty years in schools and classrooms now, I know that there are many secret signs and rituals that make up institutional life, but we are completely unconscious of the majority of them. I refer to this phenomenon as the institutional trance. When we commit to any kind of institutional organization, we enter a kind of trance state.

To the extent that we submit our individual will to the will of the institution, our autonomy is diminished. George Orwell described this very well in *1984*. He used the metaphor of loving Big Brother to describe what happens to people when they stop questioning the power structures they live in. They simply learn to love Big Brother. That is how you get along. For Orwell, Big Brother is the personification of all systems of control — government, church, school, capitalism, the family. His novel is about the importance of always remaining aware of these structures as artificial and arbitrary. He warns against the temptation of "groupthink." This is what I mean by the institutional trance. When you join up, there are certain things you are allowed to say and other things you are not. Nice people don't talk like that. Nice people don't rock the boat. Institutions love nice people. Institutions do not like what Orwell called "ownlife ... meaning individualism and eccentricity." Ownlife can lead to thoughtcrime — having individual thoughts that are not approved by the authorities. This tendency toward policing behaviour and thought is summed up in our over-use of the word "appropriate."

Schools have become very enamoured with this word, as it sounds so innocuous and yet powerful at the same time. We describe a student's behaviour or comments as "inappropriate," but inappropriate to whom? Inappropriate implies a range of what's appropriate beyond which one may not go. This range is set by those in positions of power, and the word inappropriate is usually applied to behaviours and comments that challenge the power of those in charge. This is not to say that we should not have rules and structures and order, but I do think we need to broaden the range of behaviours and activities that are permitted at school.

The Value of Talking Back

We need to broaden the range of what is allowed to be said at school. We need to permit, indeed encourage, more freedom of speech. We need to create opportunities and vehicles for kids to speak freely about what is on their minds. If we don't broaden the range of appropriate ways of speaking, students will continue to find other ways of speaking — ways we call inappropriate. Neil Postman said if you want to find out what is going on in a school, read the graffiti on the washroom walls. Today we don't need to look at the washroom walls, we have the largest, most sophisticated graffiti wall in history — the Internet. Sites like Facebook, Twitter, and RateMyTeachers allow students to say what they really think and feel about school. We can learn a lot from these comments. School provides little opportunity for talking back. In fact, it is either discouraged or punished. Why don't we want to know what students think? In post-secondary schools, course evaluations are standard. Why do we not have course evaluations in all grades? Of course there would be abuses, but if such dialogue became part of the culture of school, it could become respectful and productive. Students lash out with negative comments because they feel they have no voice. If the system regularly provided a place for students to voice their opinions, those opinions would become less emotionally charged and more rational over time. It would also get kids thinking about what it is they want as opposed to always reacting to what they don't want. Dialogue would become part of the culture of school.

A Letter from the Teacher

My grade five teacher was an eccentric older British woman who grew up in India. She had all kinds of exotic stories about diving off waterfalls in the Himalayas. I didn't know what that actually involved, but I distinctly remember the mental image. She was quite heavy by the time she came to teach our class, and I tried hard to imagine her diving off a cliff. Anyway, we were encouraged to put any questions or comments we might have about anything at all into a special box on her desk. We had a class discussion session each morning. To me this was transformational — the opportunity to talk about the process, not just be submitted to a process.

It was incredibly empowering to my eight-year-old self. I remember being frustrated with the kids who were not taking it seriously, talking and fooling around during the discussion. I wrote a letter in which I told her I was finding some of the work hard and expressed frustration about the kids who were not taking the discussion time seriously. This was her response, written in spidery cursive writing, with her home return address at the top of the page — just like a real letter.

My dear Michael,

It was nice of you to share your problem with me. Thank you.

It was not so good to hear you were having a tough time. Why? Do you find the work difficult? If you do, then please don't hesitate or be afraid to ask me for help. That's my work, and I'm always willing and promise I won't be cross.

As for the other thing. I'm trying to think out a plan where I'll be able to get the "discussers" away from the others. We'll talk about it this morning in our discussion.

Of course I won't mention it. This is between you and me only.

Your teacher,
E.A. Scott

On the outside of the folded paper, she addressed it to "Master Michael Reist." It was a thoughtful and intelligent response. It was precious to me (I've kept it for forty-five years!) because it was an acknowledgement of the value of my opinion and point of view; it was a concrete affirmation of my value as a person in the classroom. It was as far as one could get from "children should be seen and not heard." When she wrote, "I'm trying to think out a plan" it showed me that she was still working on ways to make things better in the classroom, that this was all a work-in-progress. That was very important to me, and all these years later it still is. School is a work-in-progress. We have not figured it all out yet, but we need to keep trying with the input of children.

If this kind of dialogue was more common, school would be a happier place. In a healthy home, children are allowed to express their opinions, whether positive or negative. In a healthy home, the opinions of the children are sought when making decisions that will affect everyone in the family. Why can't this be the case in school? Students would have a much greater sense of ownership and co-operation if they were included in decision-making processes. If we send our kids to school to be socialized into a democratic society, then shouldn't school be democratic?

Age-Mixing

One of the most noticeable characteristics of school is the way children are grouped by age. Ten-year-olds spend their day with other ten-year-olds. One of the ways we develop through the developmental stages is by seeing the behaviour of those further along the continuum and by interacting with them.

Age segregation is a phenomenon that began with mass public schooling. For millennia children have grown up in mixed age groups. They also had much more sustained and intimate contact with a variety of adults. In our current system a child has little opportunity to interact with children of other ages, and the main adults in the young child's life are usually one teacher and two parents. When we watch children in more unstructured settings like playing on a neighbourhood street or family gatherings, we notice that some children gravitate toward those younger than themselves while others gravitate toward older kids. School is based on the assumption that all ten-year-olds are the same. I worked with one boy in grade five who played with grade four kids at recess and pleaded to be put in their grade. Another boy who was in no way ready to handle the demands of grade three asked if he could move down to grade two. These are unusual cases because usually the social pressure to move with one's pack is strongly ingrained even by grade two or three. Children are quickly socialized to understand that school is a kind of race to the finish line and the last thing you would ever ask for is to be put back. One also quickly learns the pack rules and that the pack does not deal well with those who abandon the pack; nor do other packs (grades) deal well with new-comers.

I have known many students who much prefer the company of older kids. *The Perks of Being a Wallflower* tells the story of a grade nine student who does not fit in with his pack and ends up being befriended by a group of grade twelve students. This story expresses a reality felt by many adolescents — they do not fit in with their peer group and would like to associate with older, more mature kids. I have always found it interesting how some students will have friends outside of school who are not their age, but at school these relationships are hidden or denied. There is an unspoken rule that they will not hang out together at school even though they hang out together all the time at home.

There are also those children who enjoy or prefer the company of adults. This is common amongst only children and eldest children who tend to have spent a lot of time interacting with adults. They often feel out-of-sync during childhood and adolescence. In adulthood, their peers catch up with them and everything is fine, but, unfortunately, they feel there is something lacking in them as they grow up within a peer group with different influences. They tend to blame themselves and see themselves as somehow socially deficient, when, in fact, what is happening is perfectly natural. What is unnatural is putting all kids of the same age together and expecting them all to be at the same place.

Schools could do more to promote age-mixing. In elementary school, kids who excel in a certain subject area could spend that period in a higher grade. Children from higher grades could help out in lower grades by reading or helping with homework. In secondary schools prerequisites in certain courses could be waived to allow students to move to more challenging work. High school courses could be offered that are not grade-specific.

I taught an independent studies course in English at the grade twelve level. I asked teachers of grade nine and ten classes to recommend any students they felt were functioning beyond their grade level and were not sufficiently challenged by the junior curriculum. On the basis of a personal interview, not marks, these students would be offered the opportunity to complete their grade nine or ten English credit while participating in the grade twelve course. They would read the core works that the class was reading and discussing, and their independent work would be evaluated at their own level. What always intrigued me (but didn't surprise me) was the fact that many of these grade nine and ten students were reading and writing at a level beyond those in grade twelve.

Learned Helplessness

Socialization includes learning to be able to deal with situations as they arise, to be able to cope with the unpredictable nature of life. We talk about the phenomenon of helicopter parenting, a parenting style in which adults micromanage their children's lives in an effort to protect them from harm, but in practice it protects them from any kind of discomfort. School has been practicing this helicopter approach in its own way for decades. School is a place where a child's life is micromanaged in the interest of the smooth running of the institution. As a result, students learn to comply rather than to act independently. When one complies with the dictates of the institution, these are deemed good choices. When one does not comply, these are deemed bad choices. One quickly learns what choices to make if one is going to get along in the institution. Obedience is still the greatest value held by school. The result of all this is that we create people who don't know what to do unless they are told what to do. The reason so many kids find graduation and adulthood a scary prospect is that there will be no one there to tell them what to do. There will be no one to obey. The only person who benefits from this system is the future boss who will step in as the authority figure. In this way we can see how school serves capitalism more than it serves democracy and more than it serves the realization of an individual's full potential. In short, children at school learn helplessness. They learn that they need adults to tell them what to do. They learn that they are incapable of handling most situations alone.

The only antidote to learned helplessness is being given freedom of choice and the responsibility that comes with it. This may get messy at times. Kids may fall and hurt themselves, kids may "screw up," but that is how they learn. School has to become a place that can tolerate, indeed support, the growing autonomy of children as they transform into independent adults who can make choices and accept responsibility for them because they have had lots of practice in this from an early age. When I'm talking to parents of teenagers, I often use the metaphor of driving a car. The child has spent his whole life in the back seat or the passenger seat. It is now time for this young adult to take the wheel, to decide where he wants to go and what he wants to do.

I worked with a student who was taking an online summer school course. When I asked him what he thought of the experience, he said the main difference was no one standing over you to push you. He was required to be logged on to the site for three hours a day, and there were assignments due almost every day. As a seventeen-year-old about to enter grade twelve, he found this self-directed approach very challenging. He had been conditioned by a system that works on external motivation and when that external force was gone, he was left to fall back on his own motivation, something that was not very highly developed. In education we use the phrase, "Encouraging students to take ownership for their own learning." This is easier to say than do. Teachers easily fall into the role of task-master or overseer. Students will admit, "If I didn't have someone standing over me, I wouldn't do it." Neil Postman called this "the creed of a slave." If we were going to teach students greater autonomy and self-directedness, we would have to start much earlier and approach the project in a much more serious way. Paradoxically, for us to do this would mean doing less of what we do now — external control.

Why Do We Do the Things We Do?

It is true that no one gladly does tasks they are not interested in doing, so in addition to this element of freedom, we will have to allow choice. Here we are at the interface between individual will and social program. School is a place where the individual will must enter into a compromise with the social program of school. As a society, we have decided that there are certain core skills and knowledge that we want every student to master, *whether they want to or not*. One of the most common evening homework dialogues goes like this:

> Child: I don't want to do this. It's boring. Why do I have to do this? It's stupid.
>
> Parent: I have to do lots of things in my work that I find boring and stupid, but I do them anyway. It's just part of life.

The truth is that adults are willing to do stupid and boring things because they get paid for them. Students do not see any payoff in doing stupid or boring things. Marks are the money of school, but most students, especially younger ones, are not really interested in this form of currency, and older students know that homework completion seldom counts.

"As a society, we have decided ..." is a common expression, and one that bears analysis. When was this meeting held? Who was there? How was the decision taken? We do many things "as a society," but we have no idea why we do them or how we ended up here. Shirley Jackson's short story, "The Lottery," has been studied for decades in schools. It tells the story of a small town preparing for an annual ritual. We are not told what the ritual entails, but all the preparations are suffused with a wholesome, innocent, small-town atmosphere. It is a beautiful June day, flowers are blooming profusely, and the grass is green and lush. All the families of the town gather excitedly in the square for the annual ritual. We begin to question what is going on when people start picking up stones, but we don't really know what is really happening until the final few lines.

> The children had stones already, and someone gave little Davy Hutchinson a few pebbles.
> Tessie Hutchinson was in the center of a cleared space by now, and she held her hands out desperately as the villagers moved in on her. "It isn't fair," she said. A stone hit her on the side of the head.
> Old Man Warner was saying, "Come on, come on, everyone." Steve Adams was in the front of the crowd of villagers, with Mrs. Graves beside him.
> "It isn't fair, it isn't right," Mrs. Hutchinson screamed, and then they were upon her.

The ritual turns out to be an annual public stoning at which someone is chosen by lottery to be killed. The story was first published in 1948 and caused an uproar. Jackson had exposed the problem with the things we sometimes do "as a society." One of the things that is so chilling about the story is the absence of any individual will, any one person who speaks out and says, "this is wrong, we shouldn't be doing this." The other disturbing thing about the story is the tone of wholesomeness. The characters all seem to feel very self-satisfied just because the tradition is being followed. They like the familiarity and predictability of it, with no regard for what it actually is. We do many things as a society because "we've just always done it this way." School is one of the most obvious examples of this way of thinking.

The Hunger Games has attracted so many young people. It is a re-telling of Shirley Jackson's short story. One of the differences, however, is the divide between the adults and the children. In "The Lottery," everyone is a potential victim. In *The Hunger Games* the victims are all children. The other difference is that in *The Hunger Games* several children fight back, not just against the controlling adults of the Capitol, but even against the adult-lead rebellion whose methods the main character, Katniss, does not agree with. Katniss is a character who keeps her individual will intact in the face of institutional forces. I think this is the source of the story's fascination for young people. I think many of them feel as though they are unwilling players in a cruel form of the Hunger Games. They can't consciously name or describe the games they are forced to play, but I think, for many kids, the game of school is one of them.

4

A Closer Look at the Child in School

The Sensitive Introverted Child

Elaine N. Aron and Susan Cain have done the world a great service in raising our awareness about highly sensitive people and introverts. Elaine Aron's book, *The Highly Sensitive Person: How to Thrive When the World Overwhelms You*, focuses on high sensitivity, or high reactivity. Susan Cain, in her recent bestseller, *Quiet: The Power of Introverts in a World that Can't Stop Talking*, is interested in the topic of introversion. Highly sensitive children experience the world more intensely, on both a physical and emotional level. Highly sensitive children are sometimes called highly reactive. They are prone to allergies or asthma, and might be highly sensitive to touch, loud noises, or strong tastes. Emotionally, they feel things very deeply. Their highs are high and their lows are low. They love with great sincerity, rage at unfairness, and are susceptible to strong feelings of guilt and remorse when they transgress or even just feel they have transgressed.

Susan Cain focuses on the introvert, a psychological type first identified by Carl Jung in the early twentieth century. The introvert is a person who focuses more on the interior world than the exterior one. Introverts often have a rich inner life and like to spend a lot of their time tending this inner garden alone. For the introvert, social situations are draining. They are very content to be by themselves for long periods of time. They often have few friends and are quite content with that. These are the shy kids. We find them in every classroom. Shyness is not a disability or disorder.

Shyness is a coping strategy for the highly sensitive introvert trying to cope in an over-stimulating world. These children do not need to be fixed or changed. They need to be respected, nurtured, and protected.

The Over-Stimulated Child

In some ways, school values the sensitive introvert because they are very compliant. They are model children who sit quietly and don't make a lot of demands on the teacher. On the other hand, school is often a very troubling place for sensitive introverts, in part because there is just so much going on there. Over-stimulation is one of the most common problems we see in schools and yet it goes unidentified or not called as such. The child who withdraws deeper and deeper into his or her shell may be over-stimulated. The hyperactive extroverted child who is running around the room causing mayhem may also be over-stimulated. We need to remember just how artificial the environment of school is. When else in human history have twenty-five ten-year-olds spent six or seven hours in a room together with one adult presiding? We take the situation as normal, and we see the child who has trouble functioning within that situation as a problem. We need to reverse our thinking on this. Is the child the problem or is the situation the problem? Children have a broad range of temperaments and will react differently to this one common environment. We must learn to see their varied reactions as normal and ask ourselves how the environment could be modified to accommodate these various temperaments. Both the sensitive introvert and the hyperactive extrovert could benefit from de-stimulation in the form of time out in a quiet place.

The Teacher-Student Fit

In *Quiet*, Susan Cain quotes Dr. Jerry Miller, who says that sometimes there is a poor "parent-child fit." He tells the story of Ethan, a highly intro-verted and sensitive boy whose extroverted parents made every effort to try to "cure" him of behaviours that were simply innate to his nature. In the same way there can be a poor teacher-student fit. When the fit is right, learning can be such a positive experience. When the fit is wrong, it can be miserable. Many parents cross their fingers each September hoping desperately for a "good teacher" for their child. If we look more closely, perhaps what makes a good teacher is a good teacher-student fit. The teacher one student might hate is the teacher another student might love. Two of the most important traits to match are introversion/high-sensitivity and extroversion/low-sensitivity. As a highly introverted teacher, I think I relate much better to other introverts. These students feel comfortable in my class because our temperaments are so similar. The atmosphere created by an introverted teacher is very different from that created by an extroverted teacher. Each type also uses very different approaches. The introverted teacher is more likely to do more chalkboard didactic teaching whereas the extroverted teacher is more likely to engage in whole-class activities and is comfortable getting kids talking, out of their seats, and moving around. I dreaded group activities as a child (and still do). I would much rather sit and listen, talk one-on-one, or engage in my own independent learning. Susan Cain tells us that this is very typical of introverted, highly sensitive children. They are easily overwhelmed and prefer to take things in at their own pace, which is often slower and more reflective. They like to sit with ideas and go into them deeply. The extroverted child prefers lots of novelty and personal engagement. He is comfortable with the random, unpredictable nature of large groups. Introverts are content with solitary activities or working with one or two others. As the size of the group increases, introverts tend to turn more inward for self-protection. Both ways of being are valid, but we can see huge implications for the classroom, especially depending on the temperament of the teacher since they are the ones who set its tone and pace.

Why can't children or parents have a say in who they have for a teacher? Why is this seen as so radical or controversial? The official answer would be that it is important for children to be exposed to all kinds of people so they can learn to cope. Our job is to challenge kids to expand their repertoire beyond their comfort zones. The unofficial answer is that we have a fixed number of teachers, and we wouldn't want to end up in a situation where one teacher was being requested by everyone. If we let in the human element of popularity, respect, or choice, this would not fit with our current mechanistic approach. There are three grade five teachers. There are seventy-five fifth grade students. The computer will divide them into three groups of twenty-five each. It's clear-cut and simple, and gets rid of all the messiness of choosing who would go where and who would work well with whom. While it may be too cumbersome to create a match-making system, we should at least be willing to bring a more human approach to those kids at the extreme ends of the spectrum. For the extremely introverted, highly sensitive child, the rough and tumble, activity-centred, group-work-oriented classroom can be nothing but a place of constant anxiety and stress. Some would say this is exactly what the child needs to "cure" her of her tendencies. This is wrong thinking. As Susan Cain says, the cure becomes worse than the disease. The child suffers chronic stress, her health suffers, her learning suffers, and her self-esteem suffers. Likewise, the active extroverted child who the computer matches up with a quiet, sedentary, chalk-and-talk teacher will have a terrible year, and will probably spend a lot of time in the front office. What ends up being labelled a behaviour problem could just as easily be seen as a bad teacher-student fit.

We could do a better job of matching students and teachers. When a plane takes off from New York City, a difference of one or two degrees in its initial direction will determine whether it lands in London or Paris. A teacher can make all the difference in a child's life — for good or bad. As the twig is bent, so the tree will grow. There are many students who are "bent out of shape" by school. They are distorted and deformed and never achieve their full potential. Others are lucky enough to find the right conditions and flourish. It should not be a question of luck.

The Bright and Gifted Child

It is sometimes said that the brightest students don't learn *because* of their teachers, they learn *in spite* of their teachers. The assumption is that because they are naturally intelligent, they will learn naturally. While there is some truth in this, it must also be said that there are many bright students who do not realize their full potential simply because they never experience the right conditions. In nature, there are many seeds that will not germinate unless a particular combination of conditions exist: moisture, temperature, amount of light. When the right conditions come together, a beautiful flower will pop out of a crack in the sidewalk. This is analogous to the situation of the student.

60

Looking back over my own educational experience, I can identify times when the right teacher appeared at the right moment and said the right thing, and I know I grew because of this. I can also think of barren times when there was no one there to push me that little bit further, to encourage a budding interest or talent. This is the mysterious alchemy of teaching and learning. It cannot be programmed by any institution, but it is very important to be aware of the phenomenon. We must do whatever we can to identify a child's strengths and encourage them. Sometimes we are more concerned with identifying and correcting deficits.

The bright and gifted student finds him or herself in a system designed to serve the greatest number possible. This means the creation of a kind of grey middle where the work is not too hard and not too easy. We want to get as many through the process as possible, so the outcomes are geared to the largest part of the group that will hopefully be able to achieve them. I have met many students who were capable of far more than they were required to do. They never felt the full power of their intellect because they were never challenged to use it. As a society we are experiencing a huge loss of human potential or human capital. Many of these extremely bright kids turn to complex role-playing games or fantasy-based war games just to exercise their minds! They have memorized the long and complex backstories to these imaginary lands. They are adept at reciting and adhering to the many complex rules that need to be followed.

This kind of mental effort once went into knowing classical literature like the Iliad and the Odyssey. It went into knowing Arthurian legend. It could also be channelled into history and physics and math. Some bright and gifted students know everything about the history and politics of their virtual world but nothing about current events. They study the language and mythology of their fantasy world but avoid the study of any real foreign language or contemporary literature. When the brightest and the best are lost to us, we should all be concerned. They have turned to this more stimulating virtual reality out of sheer boredom with the handouts and worksheets of school.

Some school boards and individual schools have done a good job of creating special classes for gifted students, but there are many who do not make it into these programs, either because their giftedness is only in one area or it is simply never recognized.

We can also talk about latent or dormant gifts that lie hidden within children. How do we discover these? When a child is given the freedom to pursue his or her own inclinations, these innate gifts will naturally emerge. And I mean radical freedom. As soon as we try to systematize anything, we lose the path. As William Blake said, "Improvement makes strait roads, but the crooked roads without Improvement, are roads of Genius." When we listen to the greatest minds and those who achieved great things in our culture, one common denominator seems to emerge: "I was left alone." "I followed my own path." "I was given the freedom and time to do what I needed to do." Albert Einstein felt that one of his greatest accomplishments was surviving the processes of school with his curiosity still intact. Of course, he eventually became a pillar of the academic community, but only at a high level where his degree of specialization was valued by the group. It is during the early years of wondering and wandering that students need our support. But how do we systematize this?

One way would be to give teachers greater freedom in differentiating curriculum. On a practical level, this would entail far more work for the teacher and resistance from parents and students who believe that fairness means treating everyone the same. The school of the future is going to have to attract teachers with a very different paradigm, or they are going to have to instill it in teachers — a much more difficult proposition.

We also need to have teachers in our schools who are truly expert in particular areas, or we are going to have to find a way to access those kinds of mentors in colleges, universities, or the workplace. Sometimes the intelligence and general knowledge of the student surpasses that of his or her teacher. Young people need to have access to mentors who can lead them to the next level, or they simply need to be left alone to go there themselves. This requires time and space for the student and flexibility on the part of adults who cling to their prescribed courses of study.

The Child Who Has Trouble Paying Attention

The child who really requires time and space is the child with poor attention control. This is a growing area of concern as more and more kids come to school from cyberspace, a place of constant novelty and visual stimulation, to a world of talking and reading and writing. Attention and focus were once thought to be a single phenomenon controlled by the prefrontal cortex. Scientists are now making a distinction between the part of the brain that can focus and concentrate (a higher level activity), and the part of the brain that is easily distracted, that notices things quickly, and is able to identify threats and respond to them fast (an older survival function of the brain). Video games and other screen activities provide a strident workout for this distractible part of the brain. The frontal lobe, the place of concentration on a single task and the application of a number of skills to accomplish a goal, gets less of a workout. As a result, we get kids who are good at being distracted but not so good at focusing.

The two main types of distractibility we see in schools are visual and auditory. Kids who are overwhelmed by all they see happening around them and kids who are overwhelmed by the noise. The common denominator is being overwhelmed. In this situation, concentration is not possible.

The solution is de-stimulation — moving the child to a less stimulating environment and allowing his central nervous system to settle down. Overriding the visual or auditory sense with some other sense is also an effective strategy. Ironically, students who experience auditory over-stimulation can be calmed by something like listening to a familiar playlist on an iPod. The auditory inputs in the classroom are random, unpredictable, and potentially threatening. The student is constantly alert to multiple auditory inputs. When they put their iPod on, the cacophony of the external environment is replaced by a kind of white noise from the child's point of view. Children who experience visual distractibility can be calmed by a white or monotone study carrel or watching a very simple and calming scene like an aquarium. The child who experiences tactile distractibility can be calmed by squeezing the hand or lying under a heavy blanket. Some kids feel calmer when they are wearing their heavy winter coat because it satisfies their tactile need.

Issues with attention are strongly linked to impulsivity. When a child is overwhelmed by sensory stimuli, the impulse control center is simply not able to work as well. Imagine each sensory input being a ping pong ball coming at you. For the highly distractible child there are many ping pong balls coming in. It reaches a point where the child can no longer hit each ball back, so he simply lashes out in the form of some kind of impulsive behaviour. The classroom is a very stimulating place. Most kids learn to hit all the ping pong balls or they learn to just ignore a lot of them. They filter out stimuli in order to survive. As mentioned before, highly sensitive children do this in order to survive emotionally. We call it being shy or introverted or withdrawn. This is one way of coping with over-stimulation that is quite agreeable to the teacher. Highly sensitive children who are over-stimulated "act in." Children with poor impulse control who are over-stimulated "act out." Children who act in hardly get noticed. Children who act out get into trouble and end up being labelled as bad and, finally, see themselves as bad.

The most counter-productive response to impulsive behaviour is to treat it as a discipline issue — as though the child has *chosen* this behaviour. A common comment heard from adult authority figures when talking about a child they are disciplining is, "He made a bad choice." The way we respond to our environment is not usually a choice. It is more often a reflex. This is especially true for younger children who have not developed the ability to self-monitor, much less self-regulate. We don't say highly sensitive children *choose* to be shy. It is their reflexive response. As children mature, they become better able to consciously modify their response, but for some kids this is a huge task and does not develop until much later. It is the job of the adult in the situation to understand what is happening and to deal with it logically, not morally. The child is not being "bad." The child is having trouble coping in his environment. The simple solution is to modify the environment, most effectively by providing an alternative environment. This can mean having a blocked-off corner of the classroom or a time-out room somewhere in the school. The downside of this approach, however, goes back to the pack mentality issue, that if anyone is being treated differently, it is either favouritism or some form of punishment. We have an overriding sense in education that all children must be treated the same, and when any kind of special attention is paid to one, this becomes problematic.

Some schools have set up classrooms that function as alternative environments, and students are free to move between these environments. There are rooms in which students can read while walking on a treadmill, sitting on a balance ball, or lying on the floor under a weighted blanket. Rooms where the lights are dimmed, where music is playing or which are totally silent, or where they can stand at stand-up desks to write. The list of possibilities is endless.

The only criteria we need to use in deciding whether to employ such techniques is whether the work gets done. While it is true that these alternatives may have their own distractions and pitfalls, it would be up to the adults in charge to create the kind of structure in which this freedom could take place. The biggest hurdle would be to *normalize* such arrangements. Both teachers and students who have been institutionalized to believe that sitting quietly writing at one's desk is the norm will have to expand their definition of what "doing your work" and "being good" mean. When a teacher offers a student an alternative setting, this is usually interpreted as a punishment or that the teacher is trying to get rid of the student. As we evolve toward an educational system that is founded more on accommodating differences, we will move away from the notion that being treated differently means you are bad, have a learning disability, or have some kind of disorder.

The Positive Side of ADD/ADHD

Attention deficit/hyperactivity disorder has three main symptoms: distractibility, impulsivity, and hyperactivity. One of the best writers on the topic is Edward Hallowell. In his books he talks about the positive aspects of ADD and calls for a change in our thinking about the subject. We can call a child who appears distractible by the more positive adjective: curious. A child who appears impulsive we could just as easily call spontaneous. And why not reframe hyperactive as energetic? The language we use reveals our biases: distractible, impulsive, and hyperactive all have negative connotations. They also all imply a positive contrasting word: single-focus, obedient, still. It is clear that this bias comes from school. In many other contexts these attributes would be a liability. There are many situations where the ability to take in multiple inputs simultaneously or to switch between multiple inputs, and the ability to respond quickly and move quickly would be far more advantageous. One of the most obvious environments in which this is true is the world of business and entrepreneurship. Many of the most successful entrepreneurs of our age report being completely bored with school and diagnose themselves as ADD/ADHD. While they were able to put their "gift of ADD" to good use as adults, they often report a huge loss of self-esteem that resulted from their constant sense of failure and inadequacy in the school system. Some had the resilience to overcome this and redefine success by harnessing the innate power of their natural tendencies. Others accept the judgements passed on them by the system and never achieve their potential.

What's Your Problem?

For many kids with ADD/ADHD life is a daily barrage of negative responses. Because boys are not as good at reading facial expression and tone of voice as girls are, boys often find themselves facing an adult who has just "lost it." The boy responds honestly, "What's your problem?" not realizing that this is exactly what the teacher would like to say to the boy. The boy did not pick up all the early warning signs that a blow up was coming. The boy's inattentive, impulsive, hyperactive behaviour distracts, disturbs, and disrupts the agenda of the teacher. She tries to deal with it through subtle comments, tone of voice, and facial expression. From the teacher's point of view it is very obvious what the problem is. From the boy's point of view, there is no problem. He is simply being himself. This is another common characteristic of kids with attention issues, especially when they are younger — they are not able to self-monitor or self-regulate. They are not able to see themselves objectively within the social situation of the classroom. They are simply not aware of the effect they are having on the smooth functioning of the group. I have often thought it would be interesting to video tape a classroom scene where a child was being disruptive and show it to the child as a teaching tool in the skill of self-monitoring. We need to self-monitor before we can self-regulate. Mirroring is one strategy a teacher or parent can use. This simply involves describing the situation to the child while the child is in it.

> "I see all the other kids cutting out stars, and I see you walking around."
>
> "I am at the board explaining fractions to the class and you are taking your pen apart inside your desk."
>
> "I am almost ready to get into the car and you are still in your pajamas."

66

This kind of "reality therapy" can be very helpful to the child, but it is important that it remain an objective description and not a nagging criticism.

Having worked closely with children and teenagers with attention issues, there is one common denominator that has always impressed me — resilience. These kids have an incredible ability to bounce back. They don't seem to lay the moral judgements on themselves that the adults around them often do. "You just need to try harder." "You need to pay attention more." "You need to apply yourself." The list of pejorative sentences would be a long one. By the middle of high school, when kids really begin to see the connection between academic success, economic success, and social status, the corrosive effects of these negative comments begin to take their toll. This is when we see kids with ADD/ADHD give up. Unfortunately, it is also a time when drugs and alcohol become part of the child's landscape, and these become a form of self-medication for the growing sense of disappointment and inadequacy the child feels.

We must do everything we can to help these kids at as young an age as possible. When we see that a child has poor attention or impulse control or when a child has a huge kinesthetic need, we must accommodate these differences, not punish them! These kids make up a disproportionate number of those lined up outside the principal's office, outside the unemployment office, the social assistance office, and even in our jails. We must face the fact that the pathway to marginalization often begins in school in the very earliest grades. School is made up of winners and losers, good kids and bad kids, and once you've spent long enough in the bad kid category it is very hard to get out of it.

Medication for Attention Issues

There is a broad range of opinion on the use of medication for attention control issues, all backed up with scientific evidence. I have seen medication be a tremendous help to some kids. I have also seen it sedate and dull energetic, sparkling kids. The issue of ADD/ADHD brings A.S. Neill's question to the fore once again: Do we make the child fit the school or do we make the school fit the child? In the case of learning disabilities, we have done fairly well in the past few decades to accommodate the special needs of students who learn differently or who have difficulty with some cognitive functions. When it comes to attention and impulse control, we have done much less. We still treat it as a moral issue. In many situations, we are still operating under a kind of Victorian morality of "spare the rod and spoil the child." The rod has been replaced by low-level emotional abuse in the form of criticism and low-level physical abuse like spending the day sitting in the office without recess. The rod has also been replaced by medication.

Many parents turn to medication in order to stop the negative cycle of getting in trouble, feeling bad about yourself, and getting in trouble again. Medication can make you more "normal" — that is, it causes you to behave in ways that do not disrupt institutional decorum. The payoff can be huge: better marks, greater social acceptance from peers, and the positive regard of adults. But the fundamental question remains: is the child the problem or is the situation in which he is being asked to function the problem? Quite simply put, it is easier to change the child than it is to change the situation. A pill every morning is much easier than changing the setup of the classroom, the curriculum, pedagogical approaches, and the mindsets of adults.

A common rebuttal to the idea of accommodating the special needs of the child is this: "When he gets out into the real world, he's going to have to learn how to cope with things he doesn't like. The real world will not be willing to accommodate itself to him. He needs to get used to it as soon as possible." There are two replies to this statement.

First of all, when the student leaves school, he will have the freedom to look for the kind of job that fits with his nature. He will most likely not end up in a job that involves sitting at a desk for hours at a time doing math problems, writing paragraphs, or trying to memorize facts from text-books. He will seek out jobs that involve lots of walking around, attending to many inputs simultaneously, and being able to deal with constant novelty and unpredictability. The qualities that were a liability in school will become an asset in the workplace.

Secondly, the fact that adult life might be hard for this child is no reason to begin the hardness in childhood. We could create a positive experience that builds the child's self-esteem in such a way that when he leaves the school to go out into the real world he will be strong and capable. Instead, we often do so much harm to these kids that we send them out into the world more wounded than they were when they came to us. Our job in school should be to take children where they are, identify their strengths, and build on them. We spend too much time trying to "remediate" weaknesses, which turns into trying to beat those weaknesses out of them.

For most parents (and children when they are involved in the decision), medication is simply a practical solution. We don't have time to wait for the system to change. We need to get through this year. We need those marks to improve right away. On the behavioural side, for the child who is falling into the "bad kid" category, who is constantly being reprimanded and sent to the office, his parents' fear is justified. They want him to be able to get through the day without all the negative feedback. Medication can help with this.

Boys at School

It is well-documented that boys are not doing as well as girls in our schools. Changes are needed in the ways we approach male learners, and this change will happen when educators learn more about the special needs of boys in the classroom. We need to make learning a more positive experience for all kids, but especially for boys who seem to develop a greater aversion to school faster. If the observations I talk about lead adults to be more empathetic and therefore make better decisions about how to deal with boys in particular situations, then I have achieved my goal. I have delivered over a hundred workshops on gender differences in learning, and the most common email I get from mothers and female teachers goes something like this: "Thank you for the information you presented. I understand my son/male students/husband much better now. I have changed the way I deal with them in particular situations, and we are getting along much better now." That is all the proof I need that a few simple ideas can have a big effect for anyone who works with boys.

The Year-and-a-Half Difference

On average, there can be up to a year and a half difference in biological and cognitive development between boys and girls. Girls, on average, develop and mature faster. This has huge implications for our curriculum-centered, outcomes-based classroom where a single topic is presented in a single way and the outcomes are measured according to a single yardstick. I have used the metaphor of testing apples for redness. Not all apples turn red at the same time — in fact some apples do not turn red at all! If we judged all apples on their redness on one particular day, many apples would not "pass." This is what happens in school. There is a huge diversity amongst students, and one of these diverse characteristics happens to be gender. If boys and girls, who develop at different rates, are being tested for the same skill, in the same way, on the same day, those who are on a different developmental timeline (boys) are not going to benefit. In addition to this, because the evaluation usually takes the form of some kind of pencil and paper activity, boys, whose writing skills may not be at the same place as those of the girls, are at a distinct disadvantage. The trajectory we set for a child at a very young age can determine their future direction. Many boys in the primary division in particular conclude quite early that they are not as smart as the girls. They see themselves as poor readers and writers, and this self-perception becomes a self-fulfilling prophecy. Parents, teachers, and boys themselves need to understand that they are on a different developmental timeline.

Add to this possible year-and-a-half difference the common situation of a December-born boy sitting beside a January-born girl. Now the difference is even greater. We see the huge range again at puberty, which girls enter much sooner than boys, and even among boys the range of onset can be anywhere from ten to fourteen years old.

Parents and teachers need to be aware of this phenomenon and take it into account when assessing the academic performance or the behaviour of a boy. Boys can often appear behind academically or immature behaviourally when compared to girls. This is one of the most cogent arguments for single-sex classrooms or single-sex schools. When you have a single-sex group, the range of academic performance can be much smaller than in a co-ed classroom. The tone of the classroom is also quite different and the kinds of behaviours one sees and the methods one might use to address these behaviours are all different.

When boys do not perform at the same level as girls, we should be cautious about jumping to conclusions about their intellectual ability or their future prospects. In our highly competitive world, parents can become quite obsessive about academic performance before these grades have any practical significance. Your child's grade two marks will not determine his acceptance into law school. "Yes," replies the parent, "but I don't want him to fall behind now. He's got to keep up." I think what can do more damage is the ringing of alarm bells before it is necessary. The child who is perceived as having a problem will be more likely to develop a problem because he has been told he has one.

I am not talking here about children with true learning disabilities, and, yes, these need to be diagnosed, but I have often seen developmental differences labelled as disability — especially before the age of seven.

The Late-Blooming Boy

When the crocus blooms in April, we don't call it gifted. When the Michaelmas Daisy blooms in September, we don't call it learning disabled. Every flower has its own nature, its own timeline. We love this about flowers. Why do we have this understanding about flowers, but we don't always have it about children?

Our educational system has become very curriculum-centred. We impose a grid over these organic beings called children, and when the grid doesn't fit, we say there is something wrong with the child.

When a child is not at the same developmental level as his peers, the adults in the child's life need to show particular care and understanding of this phenomenon and not say or do anything to feed into the false idea that the child is somehow disabled or deficient, or, to use worse language, slow, lazy, or stupid. The child may simply be on his or her own developmental timeline.

It is important to explain these differences to the child. We can use the flower metaphor. Everyone develops at a different rate, and boys and girls particularly tend to develop at a different rate. Explain to the child that everyone in the class has a different birthday and some kids may be almost a year older than others. This is particularly relevant if your child is born in the last, say, third of the year. You can also use the parallel situation of physical development. Everyone in the classroom is a different height. Brain development is just like body development. Everyone is different. Don't compare yourself to the girls in the class; in fact, don't compare yourself to anyone else in the class. Your job is to move along your own path, whatever that may be and however fast or slow that may happen. Albert Einstein was thought to be slow by his elementary school teachers. I have seen countless examples over the years of students who were behind one year being in front two or three years later. It's unfortunate that the race metaphor is so prevalent in our thinking about school. It's a great metaphor for the racers who are always out front, but a discouraging one for the others.

What Can I Do to Help My Child?

As a parent, you are a constant support to your child. You are a constant positive voice in his ear. You have complete confidence that eventually he will be able to do the things his peers can do. Your default assumption is one of ability, not disability. You never communicate frustration, anger, or fear about your child's performance. You do not have the attitude that this is an emergency, a problem, or a crisis. The child will take his lead from your attitude.

As a parent, you are always working on the skills that are not fully developed in a fun, natural way. We need, first of all, to create a rich language environment for the child. There needs to be lots of talking and being read to. Higher language skills begin with simple language processing — taking in what is being said, making sense of it, and responding. Dialogue with the child is essential and implies two-way communication — engaging your child in conversation, and actively listening to what he or she has to say. This is the foundation of language facility. Let them describe at length the event that happened or the thing they saw. Let them take the time to explain how they did something. This is an important practice. There are so many word games that can be played in the car. Guess what's in my head is a great one for logical deduction and categorization. One person thinks of a word and the others take turns asking questions that can only have yes or no answers. Is it a plant? Is it an animal? Does it have fur? Do people own them as pets? And so on.

Speaking leads to reading: decoding letters, groups of letters, words, and sentences. It has been estimated that approximately half of all English words follow phonics rules and another third have only slight variations. Also there are about one hundred words that make up approximately half of all written material in English. These facts make the study of phonics and the mastery of sight words an important place to start. Sight word flash cards are readily available at most drug stores or department stores. When working with a child on pre-reading activities, the following process applies:

1. Graphemes: forming letters physically with a pencil.
2. Phonemes: knowing the sound that each letter makes.
    a. For the consonants, only c and g have two sounds. You can hear them in the words success and suggest. All the rest have only one sound.
    b. Consonant blends are next: ch, sh, th, etc.
    c. The vowels are the tricky part. Start with the short and the long ones (can and cane, mat and mate). I call the long vowel words "smiley face words" to emphasize the silent e at the end, and I get the child to draw the smile from the vowel to the silent e. For example: make, bike, home, mule.
    d. Vowel digraphs come later (rain, meat, boat). Here the rhyme is "When two vowels go out walking, the first one does the talking."
    e. The really odd ones like eight and straight just have to be memorized. English is an old and eccentric language with influences from many languages and time periods.

We begin by reading to the child for the sheer pleasure of the story. We slowly transition to the child reading a few words, then a few sentences, then a whole page. When working with a reluctant reader, we are always watching that frustration threshold. We want to push it higher, but we don't want to sabotage the pleasure of the story. The child's frustration level will vary from day-to-day depending on their mood, whether they are tired or not, and how well things went at school that day.

Many kids experience delays in graphomotor development — the simple ability to physically form letters on the page, and, later, the ability to get one's thoughts down on paper. Of course, the screen and the keyboard are revolutionizing this area, but in the early years of elementary school, printing is given great importance. We can support our kids at home in this area by drawing, first in large format, on a chalkboard or whiteboard, and eventually moving to smaller formats, on a piece of paper. Letters are really just simple pictures. If we can play with this idea, by turning letters into things — an S becomes a snake and an M is really two mountains — then letters become less of a mystery. All letters are based on lines, circles, and triangles. The neuropathways for graphomotor function are developed through use. Drawing is a good place to start.

What Can the School Do to Help My Child?

Most parents do not have the training or the confidence to look at a child's cognitive skills and determine if there is a genuine problem. Once a child's skills begin to fall far behind those of his peers, a parent may wish to have a psycho-educational assessment done. These tests can be very thorough and can tell the parent a lot about the child's current cognitive functioning. In some jurisdictions schools will provide this service if the child qualifies. Otherwise it can be done privately. I have often thought I would like to have a psycho-educational assessment done. I would be very curious to have my strengths and weaknesses calibrated in numbers and find out what percentile I fall into. The reason I can say this tongue-in-cheek is because the results would not have a significant bearing on my self-concept or my path in life. I have found work that fits well with my cognitive and behavioural profile. For the child, these tests can have a significant influence on self-concept for better or worse. As for finding a proper fit within the world, once a child's strengths and weaknesses have been identified, steps can be taken to mitigate the effects of these weaknesses in the classroom and, hopefully, run with the strengths.

For example:

- If a child's graphomotor skills are significantly impaired, then oral evaluation and the use of keyboards or speech-to-text technology can be used.
- If a child's executive functioning is poor, then the adults in that child's life will know to pay greater attention helping the child with organizational and procedural steps. Just getting started can be a huge hurdle for kids with this issue.

- If a child has poor short-term or long-term memory, then evaluation based on recall should be avoided. Instead, this child needs to demonstrate an ability to find the information he needs, when he needs it, in places other than his memory.
- If the child has slow cognitive processing speed, they will simply need more time to complete a task, and the adults in the child's life need to be willing to wait longer for the formulation and expression of thoughts.
- A child who is highly distractible will need to be redirected and brought back to task through visual, verbal, and tactile cueing.

In my work with children with special needs, the five accommodations I have seen make the most difference are:

1. Access to word processing as an alternative to writing with a pencil or pen.
2. Scribing: where another person writes or types what the student says.
3. Extra time for tests.
4. Flexible due dates for assignments. (This does not mean endless extensions. It simply means allowing two weeks for an essay instead of one.)
5. Chunking: breaking a task down into parts, and doing one part at a time.
6. Cueing: bringing a child back on task with a look, a word, or a touch.

The Language We Use When Talking About Children

In the school of the future, we will have gotten rid of words like disability, disorder, dysfunction, and deficit. These words will be replaced by the word "differences." Every child will be seen to have their unique special needs. Every child will know from an early age that everyone's brain works differently, and therefore everyone learns differently. The system of education in the future will be so eclectic and diverse that it will not favour one way of learning over another. Today the school system favours the child who can sit still and read and write with great efficiency. The other skill that will get you somewhere even if you can't read and write well is working with numbers. Words and numbers — these are the two languages that school rewards, but you have to be fast. Kids who are not fast or proficient in these two areas are said to have "special needs." This label says more about the narrowness of our approaches than it does about the kids who carry the label. In the school of the future, this narrow approach will have disappeared and all abilities will be honoured and fostered. It will be a school system based on developing strengths, not remediating weaknesses to try to herd everyone through the same gate.

When a child has been identified as exceptional in some way, it is important to talk to the child about those exceptionalities. This should be done in a very objective, factual way. It is so important that no layer of shame be added. This is one of the toxic side-effects of not talking about it with the child. The child will eventually figure out that there is some difference in the way he or she is being treated or talked about. I have worked with parents who had their child tested, a diagnosis of ADD was made, and the parents asked me not to tell the child. The decision was shame-based and therefore not at all healthy. If a child was diagnosed with diabetes or asthma, we would go out of our way to explain the condition and talk about how to manage it. The same approach must be taken with cognitive differences. Knowledge is power. The more the child understands himself, the better able he'll be to manage himself in particular settings like school, home, and with friends.

Using Metaphors When Talking to Children About Their Differences

THE TRAFFIC LIGHT

Metaphors are simply comparisons or analogies. They are an excellent teaching tool with young children in particular, but they work for all of us because they are so simple and concrete. For example, when I am explaining ADHD to young children, I point to their forehead, and I tell them that there is a traffic light in there. We talk about what the three colours on a traffic light mean. Then I explain that for some kids the light is always on green. We then talk about the implications of that — going through intersections and crashing into other people. I talk to them about the need to learn to turn on the yellow and red light, to know when to slow down and when to stop. When I've had kids with poor impulse control in my classroom, I post a picture of a traffic light in the room. I casually point to the yellow light or the red light when the child is having trouble putting the brakes on. This strategy is called "cueing" and is essential when working with kids who have poor impulse or attention control.

A BIKE WITH NO BRAKES

Another metaphor I use is that of a bike with no brakes. This is particularly helpful for adults in understanding kids with ADHD. A child with poor impulse control is like a child riding a bike without brakes. Imagine riding a bike and not being able to stop it, and the faster the bike is moving (the more stimulated the child is), the harder it is to stop, and the bigger the crashes can be. Adults will often say of a child with ADD/ADHD, "They just need to learn to pay attention." Before a child can pay attention, they have to put on the brakes and focus. But what if you have no brakes on your bike? Nagging, criticizing, and punishing are not the answer. The child needs to be slowed down (de-stimulated) or the activity needs to be sped up to match the rhythm of the child. They cannot calm themselves. A bear hug or just holding their hand can be settling and reassuring. It stops the bike.

STAYING OFF THE RADAR

For older kids who play video games, I use the metaphor of staying off the radar. There are some kids who, the minute they walk into the school building, seem to be on the radar. Kids with ADD/ADHD are often very precocious, intelligent, verbal, and engaging. They get noticed. Over time, they develop a reputation, which can be bad or good, but, most important is the fact that they always seem to be on the radar. "All the other kids were doing it too. Why was I the one to get in trouble?" I taught a boy in grade nine who was constantly getting into trouble with other adults in the building. I explained to him that school was like a video game, and you avoid getting into trouble by staying off other people's radar. Whenever he had to leave the room to go to the washroom or get something from his locker, or when the class was done and I was saying goodbye, I would often say in a confiding voice, "stay off the radar," trying to give it the tone of an adventure or challenge. When his behaviour became disruptive during my class, I would simply say, sometimes without even looking at him, "Alex, you're on my radar." This was usually enough to make him stop.

THE MONKEY AND THE SNAIL

With younger kids who are having trouble with their teacher, I show them a picture of a monkey and a snail. I ask them, "Which animal are you?" They always point to the monkey. Then I ask, "Which animal is your teacher?" They always point to the snail. The image of the snail just happens to have a large snail with a row of smaller snails following behind it. Then I ask, "In this picture, who are the other kids in the class?" They point to the row of smaller snails. Then I ask, "Do you think snails and monkeys get along?" No is the answer. "Why not?" And the child can easily talk about this. But the most important question comes at the end: "Is there anything wrong with being a monkey?" No. "Is there anything wrong with being a snail?" No. So the problem is not the people involved. The problem is the situation in which two very different kinds of animals have to live in the same cage. How could the monkey help the snail be happier? By staying away from it. By being quieter around it. How could the snail help the monkey be happier? By ignoring some of its behaviour if it's not hurting anyone. By giving the monkey chances to swing from the branches. (An interesting side note is how much bodily/kinesthetic kids and those with ADHD like the *Curious George* stories. Teachers could learn a lot from "the man with the yellow hat" who has incredible patience, rolls with George's behaviour, and always puts a positive spin on whatever mischief he's gotten up to.)

Girls at School

Girls can get lost at school for the simple reason that they are good at what school asks for: sit still, be quiet, and do what you're told. Girls are rewarded for their compliance. Because of the way their behaviour contrasts with the majority of boys, they can end up being seen, and seeing themselves, as better, smarter, and nicer. This sounds like a good place to be, but if the squeaky wheels (boys) are getting all the grease (teacher's attention), girls with difficulties or those who need greater challenges are left to fend for themselves. How many bored girls sit in classrooms waiting for the other kids to catch up or even just settle down and start working? Many girls find school a frustrating place for the same reason boys do: it doesn't move at their pace. Kids feel the teacher moves too quickly through things they find difficult (math for girls, language activities for boys) and too slow through things they find easy (math for boys, language activities for girls). Many boys become frustrated by endless repetition in math once they have gotten the concept or being asked to write about the concept or give detailed steps about how they arrived at the answer. Similarly, there are girls who might need more help with math, but are bored to tears with comprehension questions about a short story when they are used to reading a novel a week on their own. Again, we see the need for greater differentiation of instruction, more student choice, and age-mixing.

Teenage Girls

All parents are concerned about their child's progress at school; however, many parents pay far greater attention to their children in elementary school than they do to their children in middle school or high school. Part of this is the natural by-product of adolescence, when the child is seeking greater autonomy from the parents and the parents begin to pull back and let the child take more responsibility for their life.

I have seen a troubling phenomenon with girls when they reach adolescence in school, especially girls who have not been performing particularly well academically. When a boy is failing at school, he will often turn to other expressions of personal power or simply escape: sports, video games, drugs, alcohol, and high-risk behaviour. When a girl is failing at school, she also looks for other ways of expressing her personal power or simply escaping from the negative feelings of poor performance. For girls, sexuality becomes a way to experience personal power and build self-esteem. She tries to bring up her grades, but it just isn't working. When the currency of grades begins to fail, the currency of sexuality can take its place. Makeup, the right clothes, and the right behaviours will raise a girl's social status in the group quite quickly — no matter what her marks are.

What makes this phenomenon so powerful is the co-operation of media and popular culture in this process. By a very early age, girls are offered an alternative curriculum with an alternative reward system. Being thin, pretty, and sexy become the new goals. Even girls who are doing well academically will sometimes sacrifice the agenda of learning for the agenda of appearances. Being "hot" becomes more important than being smart.

Girls need to be talked to about this phenomenon. If it is brought to consciousness, then at least girls will see that they are making choices. Otherwise, like so many other things in our consumer culture, it will just become the acceptable thing to do. So much of what we do in modern culture is not the result of conscious choice. It is the result of cultural pro-gramming, generally through advertising and media. One of the greatest services we can do for our kids is to get them to step outside their media environment and look at it objectively. A fish does not see the water in which it swims. Our children are swimming in an ocean of media images that send many powerful messages. The one sent to adolescent girls is: your value lies in your appearance. If you don't exhibit these behaviours or buy these products, you run the risk of social exclusion. Adolescents are seeking personal identity and a multi-billion-dollar industry stands ready to provide them with one. Modern sociologists talk about "lookism" — the idea that how you look is who you are. And like sexism and racism, you are judged by how you look.

We as adults can ask ourselves to what extent have we bought into this idea. We all swim in the same media ocean and are just as susceptible to its influence. Before we can make our kids conscious of its powerful influence, we need to become aware of it in our own lives.

We need to talk to our daughters before the process begins as well as during the years of adolescence. We can't get preachy about it or they will just roll their eyes and turn off. Schools could do a great service for girls by giving them the opportunity to get together amongst themselves, with older girls and even female teachers, and talk about the pressures they feel to be thin, beautiful, and sexy. This would be the best way to break the spell under which our daughters turn into sleeping beauties.

Children with Low Self-Esteem

Praise is a very complicated topic. On one hand we intuitively feel that praise is essential for self-esteem. On the other hand, false praise or too much praise can have a negative effect. One way to think about praise is to compare it to food. There are healthy, nourishing foods that build up our bodies, and there are "empty" foods that provide us with energy and calories but have little nutrient value. Sugar and salt are examples of empty foods. They certainly add flavour to our diet and we like them, but their long-term benefit is minimal; in fact, too much can be detrimental to our health. False praise is like sugar or salt. When praise is honest, sincere, and warranted, it is very nourishing to one's self-esteem. When praise is dishonest, phoney, and unwarranted it can have a negative effect on the receiver. The child knows, more or less, when something he has done or made is good. When something is falsely praised, our own credibility as a source of affirmation suffers. The child soon learns that we will praise anything. "You're just saying that because you're my Mom." Our praise is no longer an objective statement of truth, but a strategy we use to try to build up the child's self-esteem. We should always be wary of strategies. They have a way of by-passing authentic human relationships, replacing them with mechanistic interactions that are supposed to work according to a plan. False praise and over-praising can send the opposite message to the one intended: "Your work is not that good." "Your performance is mediocre." "I will try to compensate for the short-coming by trying to build you up so that you will believe it is better than it is and still feel good about yourself." It is a scary thought, but children usually know what we really think and they know when they are being manipulated.

When praising our children, we should stick to what is true. Whenever we use language to achieve some other purpose, that's when the problems begin. The trick is to be aware of how we are really feeling and what we are really thinking, and when it's positive, to articulate that. I cringe when I hear the word "awesome" used for trivial little accomplishments. Awesome is a pretty strong word. It leaves no sincere adjective for the truly impressive accomplishment, and it diminishes the authenticity of our language generally.

Comparing Our Children to Other People's Children

When we compare our children to other people's children, we are often comparing ourselves and our parenting to other people and their parenting. It is a natural human tendency to measure our performance by contrasting it to the performance of others. That is what drives competition. The problem is that parenting is not a competitive sport. There are no winners or losers, and there is no right or wrong way to raise a child. It is like the question "what is the best move in chess?" The answer to that question depends on where all the other pieces are. How much water and sunlight does my plant need? The answer depends on the type of plant. When we compare our kids to other kids with very different strengths and weakness and very different external forces (both positive and negative) working in their lives, we only confuse and frustrate ourselves.

When the wicked step mother in Snow White looks into the mirror and asks who is the fairest of them all, she does not get the answer she was looking for. When the mirror says Snow White, another element is introduced into the quest for self-esteem: envy. Envy is rooted in comparing ourselves to others. We learn it early. "Why can't you be like…?" "So-and-so doesn't behave like that." Sometimes it's a sibling the child is being compared to, or a cousin, neighbour, or classmate. The result is never positive. When the child responds, "Well, I'm not Theresa!" this might sound simplistic, but, like many things children say, it contains a profound wisdom.

We can look to other parents for ideas and ways of dealing with things, but we must always keep in mind that what works for one child may not work for another, and what works in the context of one family may not work in another.

What does this have to do with school? Grades and academic performance give us the illusion that children can be compared. When we measure kids, we create an inevitable situation of comparison. Are you above average or below average? This is pretty powerful language when it comes to a child's self-esteem. What does it do to a child's self-concept to go all through school being "below average" or even "average?" As parents, we are particularly well-placed to be an antidote to this kind of toxic influence. We love our children unconditionally. We see their beauty and their gifts. We must never internalize or allow our children to internalize the idea that they are "below average." We can do this by making it very clear just what school is measuring and how it is measuring it, and limiting the judgement there. You are not your marks. The more we know about how school works — both for good and for bad — the better able we will be to make sense of the information that school gives us about our children. John Holt once said that in school, we do not see children as they really are. We see them as school reveals them to us. As parents, we must see our children for who they really are and not for the judgements and measurements of the system.

First Class, Second Class, Third Class

As the baby boom moved through the factory school system in the 1950s and 60s, it became obvious that one size would not fit all. The range of ability and interest was too large to simply apply the curriculum content and the pedagogical techniques of the nineteenth century. The first attempts at differentiated instruction were made. These took the form of creating vocational or technical schools for those students who preferred practical training — working with their hands. These students were seen as heading for the manufacturing sector. There were also schools with a commercial emphasis, often training girls for secretarial work. This kind of specialization was usually only possible in larger centers where there were enough students and enough resources to support a number of schools. The traditional high school had to differentiate instruction within its own walls. This took various forms in various jurisdictions, but the essential structure became a system of levels, streams, or tracks that a student could follow. While the labels for these levels have changed periodically, they have ended up having the connotations of a class system.

The problem relates back to the idea that school is a sorting room for the social order, a training ground for positions in capitalist society. The most well-paying jobs, according to the myth, go to those with the most training and education. University is the pinnacle of this selection process. A degree is the ticket to a well-paying job. When you combine this myth with the myth of the immigrant, you end up with a potent brew. North America is a continent of immigrants. If you work hard and get a good education, you will be successful. For the first generation of immigrants who often had little education, working hard was enough. For subsequent generations, the myth included the importance of education in getting ahead. Hard work would not be enough. This ethos has permeated our culture. Every parent wants their child to do better than they did, and school is seen as the essential pathway to this goal.

In high school, the sorting becomes visible. It may have been there in subtle ways in elementary school with different reading groups and other ways of grouping students by ability, but most students were relatively unaware or indifferent to these distinctions. In high school, this all changes. Students are required to choose courses that have particular terminal points. To use the language of school, some courses keep doors open while other courses close doors. It is a very linear model. Once you are on a particular track, your options are largely determined for you. Depending on the particular school jurisdiction, it can be very hard to switch to another track. Students in grade nine begin to notice that the friends they played with at recess in grade eight are no longer in any of their classes. They slowly begin to realize that there is a ranking system. Needless to say, this can have very negative effects on a child's self-esteem.

The solution lies partly in the system and partly in social attitudes. Students should be able to move between levels. They should be able to study at various levels in various subjects, depending on strengths and weaknesses, and the system of prerequisites should not be so restrictive that pathways are blocked or doors closed. We must also create a system that is conducive to the late bloomer (and the early bloomer, as we talked about with gifted children). We all know cases of students who did very poorly at one stage of their schooling and excelled at another stage. This variety in developmental paths continues all through life. Schools need to be flexible enough to accommodate the student who is ready to learn — at whatever age that readiness develops.

The other part of the solution to the class system problem is a change in social attitudes. While the manufacturing sector is shrinking in North America, there are still many hands-on jobs that are essential to our society. The trades are the best example. We need competent electricians, plumbers, bricklayers, carpenters — the list is a long one. In a special report on America's competitiveness in the *The Economist* of March 16, 2013, the authors report that 67 percent of manufacturing firms had trouble finding skilled workers, and that by 2020 the U.S. will be short 875,000 machinists, welders, and industrial mechanics. We need to raise the level of social prestige for these jobs. We all know kids with university degrees who are working for minimum wage, but the myth of the white-collar job persists. Working with one's hands needs to be revived as a dignified vocation. School feeds the bias that dignified work involves paper and pens and sitting at desks. There is not enough prestige given to hands-on activities. Theory and memorization are given more importance than practical application.

We also need to instill in kids a more entrepreneurial attitude to their own working futures. The idea of graduating with a specific degree and being taken on by a corporation that will protect you for the rest of your career is quickly passing away. Young people are moving from contract to contract. Every person is their own small business. Students will need to choose which skills, knowledge, and attitudes they will need in the marketplace. These choices may be very linear or very eclectic. Experience and demonstrated ability or potential will also become the new ticket forward. Marks and degrees are seen less and less as indicators of potential success. Personality, which includes behaviours and attitudes, is becoming increasingly important to potential employers. Schools need to provide this more holistic and fluid kind of preparation, and kids need to work on their portfolio of accumulated successes rather than focusing on that one piece of paper — the diploma, certificate, or degree.

5

A Closer Look at the Adults in School

The Teacher Is the Key

The most important factor in determining a child's experience of school is the person of the teacher. I say the person of the teacher as distinct from the personality or techniques or knowledge of the teacher. It comes down to who that person is *as a person*. This seems so nebulous or ethereal — and it is! What makes a great teacher is very intangible. The teachers we remember were not necessarily those who followed curriculum guidelines thoroughly. They were individuals with passion who brought that passion into the classroom. When we use the word "passion" we think of a firebrand, a zealot, an enthusiastic cheerleader type. Passionate teachers can be this way, but they can just as commonly be the quiet, unassuming, soft-spoken teacher who is equally passionate about kids, their subject, and the vocation of teaching.

If we think back to the teachers who inspired us, the teachers we enjoyed being with, there is usually one common denominator — they were individuals who worked within the system yet never lost sight of their own unique nature, whatever that was. In addition, they acknowledged our unique nature and gave us permission to be ourselves. In their authenticity they showed us that authenticity was possible within a homogenizing system. They remained human. We did what these teachers told us to do, not out of fear but out of respect.

The word discipline comes from the same root as the word disciple. Discipline has to do with following someone or some set of core values.

When a teacher has an authentic set of core values, which naturally includes respect for the other person, discipline happens naturally. There is no need for the imposition of fear and intimidation; kids are happy to comply with someone they respect and who respects them. When students come to his or her class from an authoritarian, fear-based class, they respond even more strongly to whatever respect and kindness they are shown. They comply and co-operate out of a sense of respect, but also out of a simple sense of relief to spend time in a place where the atmosphere is not oppressive.

This respectful approach has its downside for the teacher when they meets kids for whom the authoritarian, might-makes-right approach has been hard-wired into their system. They have often learned this attitude at home, and when they meet the authoritarian teacher, it all makes sense. The approach is familiar. When they come into a classroom where there is respect, dialogue, negotiation, and freedom, they perceive it as permissive in contrast to what they are used to. They see the teacher as someone to be taken advantage of. Having been raised in a world where the loudest voice is the one that is listened to, they see the teacher as weak or passive. As one non-compliant grade nine boy from an authoritarian home once advised me, "Sir, you need to yell at me!"

Staying Human

I have coached and mentored countless young teachers over the years, many of whom were empathetic, sensitive, and respectful of students. They enjoyed school themselves because they were compliant and respectful. School worked for them because they were willing to submit to its dictates. When they come to teach, they are often shocked at how many students do not share this attitude! They discover a whole stratum of kids who hate school and are outwardly hostile to the authority figures there. How many well-meaning young teachers have I sat listening to, crying at the end of a hard day, when so many students resisted or even tried to sabotage their meticulously prepared lesson plan? These teachers are not natural-born yellers. In fact, they often appear even more pathetic and vulnerable when they try that approach — the kids laugh. I explain to these young teachers the social dynamic that is going on in the classroom. I tell them they are at a crossroads that all sensitive teachers face — one path leads to a hardening of your shell, a shutting down of empathy, a cutting off of connection with the students. The other path means remaining open, trying to understand things from the point of view of the students, and trying to connect with them on a human level every day. The second path is far more challenging. You will be used and abused by those who see you as weak, but even those students are the ones who will say "hi" to you in the halls the following semester. Even those students will be the ones who remember you fondly. They may put you through the wringer, but that doesn't mean they don't appreciate what you are trying to do. In fact, they are testing you. They want to see what your breaking point is. They want proof that your respect and kindness are authentic, and the only way they can find that out is by pushing the boundaries. I tell them that if you can withstand that assault, you will enter into another level with students, and with your teaching career. You might have more problems with classroom control than the authoritarian teacher, but it's worth it in the long run. Our schools need teachers who remain vitally human and authentic, and this means compassionate, kind, and respectful. It does not mean weak. The compassionate teacher is authoritative, not authoritarian. The kind teacher knows where to draw the line and how to set boundaries. The respectful teacher does not hesitate to discipline, but it is never done in a demeaning or arbitrary way.

Hawks and Doves

One way of describing the difference in teachers is the metaphor of hawks and doves. The hawks are those teachers who give a high priority to the smooth functioning of the system. They emphasize the rules and value structure. The doves are those who give a high priority to their relationships with students. They value connection over control. Simon Baron-Cohen describes this spectrum in his book, *The Essential Difference: Male and Female Brains and the Truth about Autism*. He simply describes two distinct ways of dealing with reality. He describes a spectrum of behaviour with the systematizing brain at one end and the empathizing brain at the other. Hawks are systematizers. Doves are empathizers. Hawks love the rules. They feel a sense of security, almost pleasure, in knowing what the rules are and making sure they are followed. They have great disdain for anyone who disregards or flaunts the rules. The systematizer or the hawk can feel very at home in the school setting — especially the "tight ship" school where enforcement of the rules is given a high priority. The systematizer is happiest in any environment or pursuit that values structure and order — the military, organized sports, video games, mathematics, and physics.

The empathizer or the dove can also feel very at home in the school setting simply because there are so many opportunities for personal connection. The empathizer is happiest in social settings that allow for random and spontaneous connections. The empathizer, good at putting his or herself in the shoes of another person, also enjoys one-on-one connections where they can focus on the other person and really get to know them.

Systematizers value consistency and predictability. Empathizers are comfortable with ambiguity and novelty. School is a place where there is a constant oscillation between these two poles, therefore these two very different types of teachers can both find school a positive environment. Schools need both types of teachers. We need those who will guard the boundaries and maintain social order. We also need the nurturing care-givers who look out for the needs of the heart. Students will be drawn to teachers of a similar bent. Systematizing students will respect and admire the math teacher who "knows his stuff" or the administrator who follows through and imposes the consequences they said they would. Empathizing students will bring gifts for the teacher who shows an interest in them and console the student who got in trouble.

The ideal teacher is a combination of both styles. They can impose boundaries when necessary, but they know when to relax them in the interest of fun or individual differences. They are consistent in their approach, but are willing to allow for the special case. They are predictable, but able to be spontaneous. It would be wrong to suggest that the only good teacher is a soft-spoken, gentle, nurturing teacher. We can be equally inspired and nurtured by the tough, no-nonsense teacher who demands a lot of us. The common denominator, however, is always kindness and respect.

At the extreme end of the spectrum, the systematizer becomes the control-freak bully who loves the power trip. At the far other end of the spectrum, the empathizer becomes the cool-friend-of-the-student with no sense of boundaries or authority. Because school is a system, the systematizing function holds ultimate sway. The empathizers learn to work within the system. The systematizers wouldn't show up if school was just a touchy-feely place. Because schools ultimately favour systematizers, they run the risk of drifting toward the end of the spectrum where power and control, order and discipline are valued above everything else. The voice of the empathizer is lost. Empathizers provide an antidote or a corrective to the potentially stifling effect of systems of control. The "tight ship" school can become a bullying school where fear and intimidation are used to gain power and control.

It is important for parents to be aware of this spectrum and reflect on it in four ways. First, where does your child fall on this continuum? Does your child need lots of structure and consistency? Does your child prefer activities that emphasize systematic thinking and behaviour, or is your child more comfortable with lots of freedom and unstructured spontaneous activities? Does your child take comfort from rules and order or do they find them frustrating and inhibiting? Are personal connections essential for your child? Do they need to know the teacher likes them?

Secondly, where does your child's teacher fall on this continuum and is there a good fit? If not, then you might have to do some coaching and supporting of your child. The free-spirit child matched up with the rule-bound teacher may not have a good year. Likewise, the system-loving child may feel confused and disoriented by the free-spirit teacher. Sometimes opposites work well together and the student can benefit from the balance that a teacher with a different temperament can provide. Sometimes the differences between child and adult can be a recipe for disaster.

Thirdly, the parent can ask where does their child's school fall on this continuum. Is it a school that has struck a healthy balance between structure and freedom, between order and fun, between rules and people? In short, is it a kid-friendly school? The tone of the school is determined by the principal. Get to know your principal. The approach he or she brings to the job will permeate the atmosphere of the school.

Finally, where do you as a parent fall on this continuum? If you are a systematizer, do you see your child's spontaneity as flightiness? If you are an empathizer, are you frustrated by your child's reluctance to tell you all about their feelings? Even though you are a free-spirit, your child may crave structure, routine, and predictability. He may find your spontaneity unsettling or confusing. If you feel rules and their strict enforcement are essential aspects of child-rearing, your "lover" child may interpret your punishments as contempt or rejection. What you would call logical consequences, they perceive as a personal attack from the person they love most in the world.

So often thinking about our child-rearing practices takes us back to ourselves, to thinking about who we are, our own experiences growing up, and the good and bad matches we experienced with the adults in our lives — especially our teachers and our own parents. This reflection need not be seen as passing judgement. There is no blame to be laid when there is a mismatch between brain profiles or personality types, but for the conscious parent, these are essential questions that can lead to greater understanding of oneself, one's children, and one's relationships. If mismatches lead to discord, understanding them will lead to greater harmony.

The Stressed Teacher

Our institutions are only as healthy as the people who run them. When teachers are stressed, kids suffer and learning suffers. "Two months off in the summer, two weeks at Christmas, plus March Break! How can teachers feel stressed?" Teaching is a binge and purge profession. Teachers binge on frenetic activity during school time, and try to purge themselves of all the pent up stress in holiday time. This binge and purge also happens on a daily basis.

Stress levels rise in proportion to the lack of control we feel in a situation. On the surface, it would appear that the teacher is in control of the classroom, that he or she operates as a demi-god surrounded by compliant underlings. It does not always feel this way to the teacher. They are subject to many forces over which they feel they have little or very tenuous control:

- The principal. He or she runs the school and has ultimate decision-making power. The principal can undo any decision made by the teacher. The principal is entitled to comment on the teacher's performance at any time.

- The vice-principal. He or she is a mini-principal.
- The office secretary. She manages the command centre and has control over many things — concrete and abstract — that bear directly on the teacher's daily life.
- The custodian. He has control over the physical state of the building, including partial jurisdiction over the teacher's own classroom.
- Parents. They are silent partners. A teacher often doesn't know what they are thinking or when they will come forward to make a comment, good or bad. In the early grades of elementary school, most parents have regular contact with the teacher. Some parents have more or less trouble relinquishing control over their child during the school day. Some parents continue to insist on control into the junior grades. By middle school and high school, the parent often becomes an unknown and unpredictable entity. Should they come forward, the teacher feels a potential loss of control. Many teachers feel threatened by parental comments or questions. This is an indicator of just how insecure and stressed they feel.
- Students. This is the biggest constant unknown in a teacher's life. There are twenty-five to thirty children and only one teacher. The teacher is hugely out-numbered. Each child is like an iceberg, the tip of which can be seen sitting there at his desk, but below the surface lies that child's accumulated life experience, last night's experience at home, this morning's experience getting out the door, temperament, hormones, learning style, conflict-resolution style, moods, thoughts, and feelings. Parents count down the days at the end of summer when they will no longer have to supervise their one, two, or three children. The elementary school teacher will supervise roughly twenty-five children for six or seven hours a day for the next ten months. A high school teacher will typically deal with seventy to ninety students a day.

The teacher is like the centre of the wheel in the classroom, but there are many spokes running out from that centre — each one leading to something the teacher has very little control over. One way to reduce teacher stress and make school a more fluid place would be to break down these isolated cells — classroom groups controlled by one adult — into a more amorphous structure where each student is the centre of his or her own learning, where the adult is not the ringmaster of the circus or the conductor of the orchestra or the prison guard, but one of a number of resources available to the student. In the decentred school, the teacher would not be at the centre of the wheel trying to hold it all together. Because students would be working much more independently, the centre of power and control would shift to the student.

"This Isn't What I Signed Up For"

Anger and frustration happen when an expectation is not met. A major stressor in many teachers' lives is disillusionment. "This is not what I signed up for." "This is not what I thought it was going to be." I have spoken to countless young teachers who confide that they are not happy in their jobs. They all say they love kids and they love teaching. It's "the system" they just don't feel comfortable with. One very gifted young teacher said to me recently, "I've lost my faith in the educational system." This loss of faith is more widespread than any of us are willing to admit. I hear it from students, parents, teachers, even administrators, but in the absence of a clear alternative most just learn to accept the status quo. I tell these teachers that the answer lies in the classroom, that they have much more freedom there than they realize. The teachers who feel disillusioned are usually the most idealistic. They have a strong and positive vision of what teaching could be. They know what kids need. They are passionate about kids and learning. I tell them to harness those loves and not let the machinery of school grind them down, to hold on to their vision, and live it out in the classroom, but the valid question remains: what can we do to improve the system?

One of the things schools need are teachers who did not enjoy school themselves when they were students. Most teachers who go into the profession are people who liked school and for whom school "worked." Why would anyone change something that they personally enjoyed? When these former students become teachers they are able to relate well to the students who like school. They can have a harder time relating to students who find school difficult in terms of the academic work itself, the kind of behaviours that are required, or the social environment. We need more male teachers in the primary grades who completely understand the squirmy boy. We need teachers who were diagnosed with learning disabilities who know the challenges these kids face. We need those "bad" students who spent a lot of time in the principal's office to become principals!

Much Depends Upon the Principal

The principal has the greatest influence on the school as a whole. While individual teachers may be able to create micro-climates, the principal creates the climate of the school. It has been said that a group cannot evolve beyond the level of its leader. This is one of the reasons we see so little change in schools and school boards. Creativity, innovation, and reform can only go as far as the imaginations of those at the top will allow them to go. Good leaders facilitate the creativity of those *around* them. Poor leaders try to control and contain those *under* them. Some principals see their teachers as unruly students who need to be controlled. They fear their creativity and spontaneity in the same way many adults fear those things in children. "Where will it lead?" "We can't have chaos!" "It's my job to keep a lid on things." There is much praise for the principal who "runs a tight ship," but the tight ship is often a place ruled by fear of going down in the storm. There is nothing wrong with structure, but too often structure kills freedom, creativity, and innovation. We must have freedom *within* structure.

The Principal with Two Heads

The month of January is named after the Roman god Janus, who had two heads, one facing backward and one facing forward. He was the god of time, beginnings, endings, transitions, gates, doorways, and bridges. The principal is a two-headed Janus; he has one face that looks toward the teachers inside the school and another that looks toward parents outside the school. They often feel stuck in the middle. For many teachers, the principal is seen as their defender against parents. The principal knows this and walks a fine line when a parent has a "concern" about their child. Ideally, these concerns are dealt with between the parent and the teacher, but sometimes there is an escalation, and the principal becomes involved. Sometimes the parent bypasses the teacher and goes directly to the principal. The principal becomes a kind of buffer or gatekeeper or spin doctor between the teacher and the parent. She tries to calm the fears of both, to ameliorate the situation. Often one thing is said to the parent and another to the teacher.

We all have our "front-porch face," the face we show to the world. Dysfunctional families are characterized by a huge discrepancy between the front-porch face and the inside-the-house face. In the dysfunctional school, the same phenomenon occurs. There are multiple versions of reality. The principal is uniquely positioned to break this spell, to bring competing versions of reality together to discover the truth. This would require a level of honesty and self-criticism that is sorely lacking in schools. It would also require kindness, courtesy, and forgiveness. Because there is so much fear in schools, these virtues are given little place. The default stance between teachers, principals, and parents is a defensive one. All parties are defending themselves against the fear of being hurt, criticized, wrong, weak, or being exposed as a bad teacher, parent, or principal. Face-saving takes priority over truth, and, of course, the child is the one who suffers in the end.

Like any other art, the art of communication takes practice. Communication between home and school gets very little practice. I have always wondered how staff meetings would be different if parents were present. Parent volunteers are fairly common in the primary division, and then parents slowly disappear from school. Parent observation in the classroom is seen as a breach of contract — only administrators are permitted to evaluate teacher performance. I spoke with a father whose son was having a hard time at school and he suspected that the teacher's approach was part of the problem. He asked if he could sit in. The teacher informed him that parents were not allowed to evaluate a teacher's performance. His less-than-diplomatic response was telling, "Oh, you don't have to worry about that. I've already evaluated your performance." Here's the rub. We can let parents in and create a dialogue about education, or we can retreat into our corners and create an adversarial stance where neither party benefits, least of all children. Opportunities for discussion and dialogue should be a natural part of school culture. Such dialogues would require respect, kindness and compassion. Few parents would welcome external comments on their parenting practices. It is the same with teachers. What is unique about the parent-teacher situation, however, is the fact that the teacher is like a co-parent who actually spends more hours in a day with the child than the parents do. They should not be in an adversarial position toward each other. They both have the same child's interests at heart.

6

Am I Crazy or Is the Situation Crazy?

MENTAL HEALTH IN OUR SCHOOLS

Ribbons Are Not Enough

There are three mental health issues that have a profound effect on our schools: the mental health of students, parents, and teachers. We are willing to talk about student mental health, but the topics of parental mental health and teacher mental health are largely ignored. This has to change. Our institutions are only as healthy as the people who run them.

The mental health issues of adolescents have been well-documented: depression, eating disorders, suicide, bipolar disorder. These are very trendy topics that daytime talk shows and supermarket magazines are glad to talk about because they deal with a relatively small percentage of the population. We can distance ourselves from these cases and talk about "those troubled kids." Apart from these well-documented disorders, the biggest mental health issue affecting almost every child is stress. It is much harder to talk about because it is not seen until it comes out in particular symptoms or behaviours. Many of the behavioural and academic issues we see in schools today can be traced back to stress.

So many of our social problems are dealt with in superficial and mechanistic ways: posters, fridge magnets, T-shirts, and ribbons that we are running out of colours for. This is a logical approach for a consumer culture. By buying and distributing anti-bullying products we will solve the bullying problem. It is an external response to an internal problem. Sometimes we move beyond the product-response to the event-response. We will have an assembly, a speaker, a wellness day. Sometimes the response is a memorial after the fact, and then a bench, tree, or plaque is dedicated to someone who has been lost or a cause that will go on.

These kinds of approaches, while well-meaning, are not enough. What we need in our schools are adults who are willing and able to connect with kids on a meaningful level. These are not just guidance counsellors and social workers and psychologists. They are adults who have evolved enough through their own hardships and are able to help kids through theirs — adults who understand. Working closely with young people and their emotional lives can be very messy. There is no standard procedure to follow. Roles have become very defined and specialized in our schools. Most teachers have no formal training in counselling. That is someone else's job. It is part of the mystery of human relationships why certain kids will open up to certain adults. Kids do not confide in an adult because of their job description or their qualifications. They confide in an adult with whom they feel a connection. So many kids feel disconnected and alienated. The great psychologist of childhood trauma, Alice Miller, asked herself why some kids survive their trauma and actually become stronger while other kids are defeated by their trauma. She suggested the essential difference lay in the fact that at some point the child met an "enlightened witness," someone who saw the child for whom he or she really was and saw their soul. Teachers and adults generally need to be ready to play this role with young people. They need us, and they need us to have done enough of our own inner work, so that when they come to us, we will have some kind of wisdom to impart. Ribbons are not enough. Kids need wise, caring adults who are willing to stop what they are doing and listen.

Stress

School as an institution is a contributor to stress in people's lives. School as it is now is not only a stressor for students, it is also a stressor for teachers, administrators, and parents. This is not how it has to be. Many of the issues I raise in this book, I raise because they are stressors. Restrictions on physical movement, the power of marks, being constantly judged, restrictions on individual freedom — all of these things cause stress. School should be a place where kids are happy to go. School should be a place where kids feel relaxed, where their bodies move freely, their minds work effectively, and their emotions flow smoothly.

Stress increases as our feelings of personal power decrease, when we feel we are at the mercy of forces beyond our control. This describes school well for students, teachers, and parents. Stress also leads to cortisol production. In low doses, cortisol can be stimulating, but when cortisol levels pass a certain threshold, brain activity is reduced — we just can't think or learn as well.

Two very natural feelings occur in adolescence: insecurity and low self-esteem. These are phase-appropriate feelings because the body, brain, hormonal system, and psyche are in such a state of fluctuation. Our personalities, self-perceptions, social behaviours, and social standing are all so volatile during this period of transformation. So much changes from one day to the next, from one hour to the next. We feel out of control. Stress, therefore, is also a very natural part of this period. But why do we add to it so unnecessarily during adolescence?

If we were to break down the pressure-cooker of school into a more decentred entity, we would create a less stressful environment. When we put hundreds of teenagers in one building all day, every day, for ten months a year, we are inevitably going to have problems. We create a kind of micro-society where the "rule of cool" is supreme. We never ask ourselves why kids act one way inside of school and another way outside of it, or the even more profound question: which of these two behaviours is more authentic? Which of these behaviours is healthier? We all engage in situational behaviour, but the situation of school is so prolonged that it can become a kind of second self, an artificial self constructed for survival. The great tragedy occurs when the constructed self replaces the authentic self. Mary Pipher subtitled her classic study, *Reviving Ophelia*, "Saving the Selves of Adolescent Girls." I think it would be safe to say that many people's selves are lost in school, not just those of our girls.

School should be a place where the authentic self is able to thrive. The two main forces that work against this are the concentration of so many students in one location and the application of one process to all students. The two are related — the larger the group becomes, the more standardized the approach must be. We need to find alternatives to the large-scale processing or mass warehousing of children. Smaller schools would be less stressed environments.

Fear

Another one of the main stressors affecting our children's mental health is fear. Fear of failure, fear of social exclusion, fear of appearing stupid, fear of punishment, fear of disapproval. School is a place where a child's performance is constantly being judged both by adults and peers. In the early years it is the adult's judgement we fear most. In adolescence, it is the judgement of our peers.

Teachers also experience a lot of fear in their day. Fear of the students, especially in terms of behaviour. Fear of the negative judgement of colleagues and administrators: Am I doing the right things? Am I good enough? Fear of parents: Are they satisfied with my work?

Finally, there is a fear one wouldn't expect to find at school. The fear parents feel. Will my child be successful in life? Is my child happy? Is my child normal? Will my child fit in? These fears are usually carried into the school by the child, but they originate with the parent. A child stresses over marks because they have learned from their parents that marks are the most important measure of a person. A child stresses over their place in the pecking order, academic or social, because they have learned from their parents that life is a ruthless competition and you have to get ahead of the others in order to win. A child conforms to every social norm presented because they have learned from their parents that fitting in is more important than anything else. All of these attitudes and behaviours are rooted in fear. They are all well-intentioned, and yet they are huge stressors for parents, children, and teachers.

Trust

The great antidote to fear is trust. We have so little trust in kids and their ability. We wring our hands as though we have no faith in their ability to cope with situations or achieve particular goals. We feel they need us as parents to control and influence everything in their lives. When they move onto other caregivers, those caregivers become our agents for this control and influence function. We seem to live by the unspoken motto: "My children would be nothing without me." Or "My children would be capable of nothing without school." We have no trust in the innate curiosity of our children, nor in their innate motivation. We sometimes seem to assume our child is a passive blank slate who would not act unless acted upon, and upon whom we can write whatever agenda we have planned for them. The scary reality is that people become what they are perceived to be. If you see your child as passive and unmotivated, they will become passive and unmotivated. If you see your child as the "boss of himself" he will become his own boss, and he won't need adults to boss him around and he won't need to be subservient to any bosses he meets in the future. I have seen so many cases over the years where the parent had no trust in the child and it became a self-fulfilling prophecy. The parent tries to be motivated *for* the child. This never works. You cannot be motivated for another person. You can only motivate yourself. I have seen so many students disengage because Mom and Dad are doing all the engaging.

The story of raising a child is the story of letting go, and that requires trust. We gave our child a great gift when we let go of their tiny hands as they were learning to walk and when we let go of the bicycle seat when they were learning to ride. In each case they fell, but we didn't let that stop us from trusting them to try again. This same process has to go on all through life. We trust, they try, they fall, they try again, we trust again. Eventually, they will learn to stand on their own two feet. That is what we want for them.

Our lack of trust in our children points to something even deeper — our over-identification with them. "My child is an extension of my self. If they look bad, I look bad. Their performance is a reflection on my parenting." Child psychology and parenting theories have done much to reveal the powerful influence of parents on their children, and that has been a good thing. The downside of this whole new area of study is the anxiety it creates about whether or not we are doing the right thing. Before the twentieth century, most parenting was done unconsciously. Old methods were simply repeated automatically. With modern psychology has come the idea of the right way and the wrong way. The constant question on every parent's mind is if they're doing the right thing. While it is very important to be a conscious parent, there is a danger of taking it too far and seeing our parenting as some kind of test that we have to pass, or seeing our child as some kind of entry in a contest we have to win. Life is not a race or a contest, our children are not objects, and the judgement of others does not matter.

The issue of trust plays a huge role in what happens, and does not happen, in the classroom and the school, generally. Schools trust kids even less than parents do. Children are not to be left alone, they are not to run or hold scissors. Some adults begin with the assumption that all kids are innately reckless and that their default mechanism is to show poor judgement. Worse than that, they will take advantage of you or any situation they can, so you need to be constantly on your guard against them. These attitudes end up becoming an accurate description of how kids act, because we have taught them to act this way. You get what you expect. Physicists tell us that the observer influences the phenomenon he observes. This is certainly true of children. Wayne Dyer said, "When you change the way you look at things, the things you look at change." If we see our kids as trustworthy and innately responsible, this is what we will get. What a great goal!

Trust situations like letting kids use scissors and leaving kids alone in a room together raises the spectre of that modern-day boogey man: liability. Courts use the term "due diligence." If a person does not follow the policies and procedures set out by the institution, one is vulnerable to prosecution. The more prosecutions that happen, the more rules get made. The more rules we make, the tighter we bind our own hands.

Anger

Another stressor is anger. There is much anger in our schools, in both children and adults. Anger is an important emotion to pay attention to. Most often we just try to repress it or medicate it. Anger is a message from the soul. It means a boundary has been violated or an expectation has not been met. What boundaries are violated in school? For children it is the daily thwarting of their will to power. They want to be their own masters, and at every turn they feel as though someone or something is telling them what to do. Boundaries can be physical, emotional, or psychological. Physical boundaries include the need for personal space. For some kids this is more important than others. Some kids need to have a "nest," a space they feel they have some control over. At school, there is very little sense of personal space. Think of the teenagers who are so happy to finally get their own locker. Some of them will spend hours setting it up, arranging and re-arranging it as though it was their first apartment. For elementary school children, you might see this phenomenon expressed in the ownership they take for their own desk. Sometimes this ownership takes the form of a physical "nest" of papers and debris that drives adults crazy. This is sometimes exactly what it is meant to do. The messy desk is a personal statement. It is a declaration of independence expressed in physical space. (Teenage bedrooms are the same thing.)

Emotional boundaries are much harder to see, but a lot of the anger we see in schools is caused by their violation. When feelings are not acknowledged or respected by others, this is a boundary violation. A student is feeling sad about the death of a pet or Mom and Dad fighting last night, but this morning we are going to the gym for a pep rally where we are all expected to chant and cheer and show enthusiasm. The most obvious form of emotional boundary violation is harsh words, put downs, criticism, and humiliation. These are all too common occurrences at school — coming both from peers and adults.

Anger is caused by the violation of these boundaries and by expectations not being met. One of the biggest expectations not met, especially by boys, is that school will be a "fun" place. Apart from their anxiety about the newness of school, boys and girls enter with a relatively positive expectation that this will be a good thing. Within a year or two, many boys feel that the environment of school is not conducive to who they are, that there is some kind of mismatch between what they want and what school wants. This can lead to anger and acting out of various kinds.

Unrealized expectations occur for many students every September. They come to school full of hope that this year will be different. They will turn over a new leaf and their marks will improve. They will learn to like school and do well. And then the first few tests or assignments come back and it is the same story all over again — forties, fifties, sixties — that's all they ever seem to get. Imagine going through twelve years of school and never having any marks much above sixty but lots of marks in the forties and fifties. This is a reality for many kids. It can fill them with a low-level anger that simmers over time. "What's wrong with me?" "I am so dumb. Why bother?" By high school (if not sooner), the goal becomes just to pass and get out of there, away from the constant grinding down of self-esteem. It is a rational response to an irrational situation. The stress created by unrealized expectations originates both in the child who does not feel he is living up to his own expectations, but also in his parents who feel the same way. The child can carry both stresses — his own and that of his parents.

Love

If trust is the antidote to fear, love is the antidote to anger. The very notion of love being present in our schools is seen as soft or overly emotional. As education has become more mechanistic and more of a proving-ground for children, the idea that their emotional needs be met at school is seen as a frill, an afterthought, a by-product. That would be nice, but it's not essential. I send my child to school to be taught, not to be loved. I will take care of that at home.

I mean love in the broadest sense of a deep positive regard for the other. When we love someone, we respect their boundaries. We do not try to invade their physical space, their emotional space, or their psychological space. We allow them to be who they are. When we love someone, we do not impose expectations. We love them unconditionally, not according to whether they've lived up to our expectations or not. We love them for who they *are*, not for what they *do*. Some of us were taught that love is conditional on our performance, that it has to be *earned*, and we end up passing that teaching on to our children. The positive regard of teachers and parents is often based on compliance and achievement. "I like you because you do what you're told and you're smart."

Many jurisdictions spend millions of dollars a year testing kids' academic achievement levels. Why don't we measure students' happiness levels? Why don't we test schools to find out if students feel loved, accepted, and respected? We know that mental health is essential for learning, and yet we do nothing to monitor it. When Bhutan decided to measure "Gross National Happiness" (along with the more common Gross National Product), this was seen as a quaint and charming gesture by rational Western minds, but it is a model that all countries should follow.

7

Discipline

KEEPING THE LID ON

When I went to elementary school in the 1960s the strap was just on its way out. It was still used, but the times they were "a changin" and with Kent State and the Vietnam War, explicit demonstrations of force were being questioned. It was also a time when the whole area of child psychology was exploding and reaching a mass audience because of writers like Dr. Benjamin Spock. It became clear that there was a direct correlation between the way we treat children and the way they turn out as adults. Corporal punishment was an easy target of reform, and in most jurisdictions it was eventually outlawed. What was harder to reform were the other forms of punishment that came to fill the void. The most toxic and insidious of these were words. Sarcasm, ridicule, criticism, and humiliation took the place of the strap. A teacher or principal faced with a misbehaving student, especially a chronically misbehaving student, had to do something, and this was the easiest approach.

In too many places this is still a method of discipline. It is quick and easy and gets results. There is no record of what was said and no overt actions that can be called into question. The results of such an approach are corrosive and destructive, not just for the student receiving the words, but for other students hearing the words spoken. The tone and content of these words register deeply in the hearts and minds of children. This is what the adult thinks of all of us. In this burst of anger, the polite façade has been dropped, and we feel we are hearing the truth. "I am bad." "I am stupid." "I cannot control myself." "The teacher doesn't like me." These are the sentiments conveyed. Psychologists tell us that praise registers in the frontal lobe, but criticism and anger are felt on a much more visceral level in the amygdala, the ancient reptilian brain, the fight or flight centre. When we are faced with someone's anger and hostility, the message goes deep and is remembered far more easily than syrupy praise. The anger of an authority figure, especially someone who is supposedly in a care-giving role, is perceived as a huge threat, and understandably so. This is the person who is supposed to be taking care of you. This is the person you are supposed to go to in times of threat, but right now, they look like a threat themselves! The child feels confused and vulnerable. The adults in this place are on your side, until you mess up, and then they will turn on you. This is not a recipe for trust.

When a student is non-compliant, we must ask ourselves why. If all behaviour is logical, what is the logic in the child's behaviour? Should a child be punished for being bored? Should a child be punished because it's the third day with a substitute teacher who is just giving them busy work? Should a child be punished because they have poor impulse control or have a huge need for gross motor movement? We punish many behaviours that are perfectly logical or natural.

School relies very much on the social contract — a tacit understanding that I will not do anything to harm you if you also agree not to do anything to harm me. This principle works up to a certain point. I tell misbehaving students, "You have the freedom to do what you want, but you do not have the freedom to interfere with the learning of other students or my freedom to teach the class. If you can't control yourself, then I will have to control you for you." In the best of all possible worlds this would mean removing the student from the social situation that depends upon this contract. If the student is working alone or with one other adult, then the social contract changes completely. I have seen this strategy work time and time again. It should be the standard approach for a non-compliant child whose behaviour is disruptive to the group. Simply change the situation.

For some kids, especially those still in the narcissistic stage, the ability to restrain their will in favour of the smooth-functioning of the group is just not fully developed yet. The child may be able to do this for a couple of hours, but they may need some time outside the group, to focus on their own thoughts, feelings, and motivations. Narcissism is a word that has come to have negative connotations like self-centred, arrogant, conceited, or spoiled, but all children begin their development in a completely narcissistic state. It is essential to our development to begin by strengthening and affirming the self. Eventually we pass out of the narcissistic stage and learn to accommodate our own needs and desires to the needs and desires of others — most notably the needs and desires of the group. If a child does not "complete" the narcissistic stage, for example by being drawn out of it too quickly, he will keep reverting back to it in later life. Psychologists tell us that narcissistic adults are those who did not have their narcissistic needs met in childhood. It is as though their mantra for the rest of their lives is "What about me?"

This issue of negotiating social situations is going to become a greater problem in the future as kids spend more time online, which requires minimal social practice. School is a place that requires complex social negotiations over many hours. When I'm online I can do whatever I want. It's always my turn. It's all about me. Here we can clearly see the disconnect between the world of school and the world of cyberspace. We can also see the danger of online activity prolonging the narcissistic stage.

In addition to the use of verbal punishments, another common approach to non-compliant behaviour is restrictions placed on movement. This usually takes the form of sitting in the office. It is not uncommon for a non-compliant child to spend several hours or even a whole day sitting in the office. Sometimes there is a special room allocated for this purpose, sometimes the student sits in the middle of office traffic, or, in some cases, the child will stand outside the office on public display as a kind of example to others, not unlike being put into the stocks in the middle of the market square in the Middle Ages. Many years ago, I went into a school and there were three boys lined up facing the wall outside the office. The striking thing was that they were required to keep their noses touching the wall! A more recent anecdote was the story of a misbehaving boy who was sent to the gym and had to walk around the perimeter, staying on the painted line, for one hour. These are not common approaches, but they show how much latitude administrators and teachers have when it comes to imposing "consequences."

The simple restriction of movement is probably the most common consequence for misbehaviour. What makes this so problematic is the fact that for so many of these students the need for movement and frustration with the restrictions placed on it are often the cause of the misbehaviour in the first place. We have a student who is misbehaving because he needs to move and what do we do? We take away all opportunity for movement, thus raising their frustration level, their anger level, their hatred of school, and their negative self-perception. One of the most common experiences of kids with ADHD is time spent in the office being forced to sit still. We are punishing a cognitive profile! We do not send the shy, introverted student to the office because she refuses to participate in classroom discussions. One cognitive profile is disruptive to the institution; the other is not. Both children have the right to be the way they are, and they have the right to be treated fairly in light of who they are. In many jurisdictions, a diagnosis of ADD or ADHD does not legally qualify a student for accommodations or modifications in the classroom. They are treated the same as everyone else, and yet their cognitive profile does not fit well with the demands of school. As Mel Levine said, "To treat everyone the same is to treat them unequally." Students who have a hard time sitting still or a hard time focusing for extended periods of time need to be understood and accommodated. They are not like other children, and their brain profile puts them at a distinct disadvantage for the kinds of behaviours and mental processes that school requires. If we were to study the cognitive profiles of adults who spent a large part of elementary school and high school in the vice-principal's office, as well as those who dropped out and those who got caught up in our justice system, we would find a disproportionate number with poor impulse control, short attention spans, and high kinesthetic need (also called hyperactivity). The way these adults were treated as children has a lot to do with the trajectory their lives took.

Suspension is another response to non-compliant behaviour. This is like modern-day shunning. We simply exclude the person completely from the group. Students who get suspended are most often students who don't like coming to school. Their punishment is that they don't have to come to school. The student who chronically skips class to stay home is punished by being told to stay home. It is an absurd solution to a problem that runs very deep.

To really deal with the problematic behaviour of the non-compliant student would require two things:

1. Really getting to know the student, finding out what all the contributing factors are to this behaviour, and trying to help. This approach could change the way the student experiences the institution.
2. The second approach is the most difficult. The institution may have to change the way it operates. Schools should ask, "What are *we* doing to contribute to this behaviour?"

We like to blame the victim. It is much easier than examining our own behaviour. We see the entire problem as originating in the child. The context may be just as much to blame. As a counsellor, I see the same problem arising in families. The child or adolescent is sent to me to fix. There is no willingness to see the role the parents or the whole family may be playing in the child's behaviour. We just want the child to change, not us. In so many counselling situations I have felt that the parents need the counselling much more than the child, and, if the parents were to get that counselling and change some of their behaviours, the child's behaviour would automatically improve. This is the case with school too. If we were willing to modify some of our behaviours, the behaviours (and performance) of our students would improve. Sometimes it's the school that needs counselling.

Listening

Students who are not compliant need to be listened to. They have important things to tell us about themselves and about ourselves. What children and adolescents need more than anything else is to be listened to and heard. In most child-adult exchanges, it is the adult who does most of the talking. It is a power relationship and talking can end up being a simple expression of power. Adults sometimes use talking as a form of control. As long as I'm talking, you can't, and it is clear in the conversation that my words carry more weight than yours. There is also the issue of who gets the last word. There are some people for whom this is very important and for whom it is an expression of power and control.

Children and adolescents need to be listened to and *heard*. Sometimes we will stop talking and listen, but are we actually hearing what they are saying? Are we taking what they say seriously? So often in adult-child exchanges, the adult's response is simply to point out how what the child just said is wrong or inaccurate. It is often assumed that a child's perspective is automatically limited or even flawed because of their age. We need to have greater respect for what children have to say about their own perceptions and experience. If we are not listened to, we can become depressed and confused about our own perceptions: am I crazy or is the situation crazy? Kids who are not listened to end up having a very tenuous grasp on reality. When I ask a child who is seldom listened to what they think or feel about a particular situation, they will sometimes look at me uncomprehendingly as though in a fog. They have had no practice articulating their thoughts and feelings. They have had lots of practice adopting the perceptions of the authority figures in their lives and are often waiting to be told what to think or what to feel.

Listening authentically to children requires humility. The idea that children should be seen and not heard is still present in our culture. To listen to a child is seen as treating them as an equal, and this rubs some adults the wrong way. Adults are more important than children. Children are *below* adults. This mindset is more common than we would like to admit.

In the conflict situation, children also need the experience of negotiation. This implies dialogue — give and take, back and forth. It implies finding common ground and arriving at consensus through compromise. A lot of adult-child dialogue is ultimately about who is right and who is wrong. Who is the winner and who is the loser. Discipline comes down to power and control when it should be about finding a resolution to conflict.

Natural Consequences

Natural consequences are a good method of discipline when there *are* natural consequences. Homework is a common battle fought between children and parents. Sometimes I advise letting natural consequences take their course. If you don't do your homework, your teacher will be angry with you or you will fail the next test. But there are other situations where the naturalness of the consequences is not so obvious. In fact, for the student, the consequences might be positive and serve to encourage the behaviour.

The most common example in the classroom is negative attention-seeking behaviour. The student may be seeking the attention of the teacher or the other students — the class clown syndrome. The natural consequences of this behaviour are not negative from the student's point of view. "I got the teacher to pay attention to me (even though it was negative) and I got the attention of my peers through their laughter." In this case the adult has to invoke the social contract rule: freedom ends where the rights of others begin. "I have the right to be able to teach this class, and your fellow students have the right to learn. To the extent that you are imposing on either of these rights, I have the responsibility to act." The quickest and simplest approach is to remove the child from the situation, but this only solves the immediate surface problem. The real task is to sit down with the student and find out what is going on inside. Attention-seeking behaviour is often best solved by paying greater attention!

Restorative Justice

In cases of physical or emotional harm or harm to another person's property, restorative justice should be standard practice in schools. In restorative justice, the emphasis is on the human beings involved, not the institution. "You have not just broken a rule from the rule book, you have harmed another person or the community." This is a people problem, not a mechanical problem. The victim is included in the process, as are the other members of the community.

The first question may be how to restore what was taken or damaged, but the next questions are just as important: why did you do this, and what can be done to prevent this kind of behaviour in the future? Restorative justice sees the school as a community of relationships rather than a disembodied institution.

8

Marks

THE MONEY OF SCHOOL

Marks are the currency of school. They are what you get paid with, and you use them to move up to higher levels within the economy. Report cards are like financial statements: a report on your value. Some students are very rich, others quite poor. There are two disturbing things about the economy of school that are also true of the general economy. First, the rich get richer and the poor get poorer. Secondly, the have-nots far outnumber the haves. Kids who start out with high marks generally stay at that level. Success breeds success. Sociologist Robert Merton called it the "Matthew Effect" based on a line from the gospel of Matthew: "For whoever has will be given more, and they will have an abundance. Whoever does not have, even what they have will be taken from them." Once a child perceives him or herself as smart and once the adults in that child's life do the same, the die is cast. That child is much more likely to be successful. Similarly, the child who starts out with low marks is more likely to stay there. These social markers are so powerful. As the rich are often accused of having a sense of entitlement, so too the smart child ends up feeling entitled to his or her success. It is a heady place. Likewise, the poor are often spoken of as marginalized. This word could be applied to students who consistently achieve low marks.

The world's wealth is concentrated in the hands of a few. There is a call for greater equality and sharing of resources. This same phenomenon exists in education. The system favours an elite group who come out on top. The rest are left to fend for themselves. Capitalism is based on myths like hard work equals success, the rich worked for what they got, and anyone can be a millionaire. We know that these statements are not always true. The system is not just. It favours some over others. It does not have the interests of people at heart. It is a system that serves itself and tolerates no criticism. The same analysis can be applied to school. The need for school reform is as much a social justice issue as that of reform to the economy. In fact, the two are intertwined since schools serve the economy.

On one hand we want to know how our child is doing, and we find this out by comparing him to his immediate peers or by comparing him to a broader statistical norm. This can be helpful information when we want to know what our child's strengths and weaknesses are. On the other hand, we all know the effect marks can have on self-esteem. Low marks can have a very corrosive effect. We would like to think that they are motivating, but in most cases they are only discouraging. Getting consistently high marks can have negative side effects as well. Students with high marks often walk a tight rope of performance-based esteem, wondering when they will fall. Students who get high marks from a very young age have nowhere to go but down. It can be a precarious feeling.

One of the biggest problems with marks is the arbitrary nature of the moment we take the snapshot. For example, if we take a snapshot (evaluation) of the child's ability to read fluently in the middle of grade two, there will be a huge range of ability at that moment. If we were to take the snapshot of the same group of kids one year later, most would have met the standard requirement. The lower grade two mark only tells us that the child is not there *yet*, not that the child is behind or deficient. One child gets an A because she was *there* in her reading development; the child who got a C or D may just not be *there* yet.

We take children who are on different developmental timelines and hold up a standardized yardstick to measure their development. We talked earlier about the plight of the December-born child. They are being evaluated and compared to children who may be eleven months older — a huge difference in the primary grades. In his book *Outliers*, Malcolm Gladwell describes the many advantages that come to the January-born baby. When we segregate kids by chronological age, we are always going to have a huge range of ability because our groupings contain twelve months of development. Over time, those at the higher end will have what Gladwell calls, an "accumulative advantage." Tutoring companies have mushroomed in the past few decades capitalizing on this phenomenon. The child who is not there yet is put through extra drills in the hope that he will catch up to his cohort. It is like trying to make a Shasta Daisy flower at the same time as a Black-eyed Susan daisy. Yes, they are both daisies, but they are different. Having worked both in the classroom and individually with kids for over thirty years, I have seen time and time again the child who didn't have the skill at one point in his development blossom in that skill later on. On the other end of the spectrum, I have seen many kids labelled as gifted in elementary school who were simply ahead of their cohort, and when the group caught up with them, the giftedness "disappeared."

My heart goes out to the child who is not on the same developmental timeline as the top end of the class. He can be doomed to perpetual low marks and perpetual disappointment because as children move through the grades, the bar moves too, and they can just never catch up. In several cases I have counselled parents to hold the child back a year. In each case, the school was unwilling to do this. Notice our negative language of holding the child back — a better expression might be to choose a more appropriate group for him. I worked with one grade three child who desperately wanted to repeat the year and a grade six child who played with the grade fives at recess and repeatedly asked if he could be put in that grade because, as he said, "I feel more comfortable with those kids." The potential problem with this approach is the fact that child development does not always follow a consistent rate. You can have a child who might lag behind his peers for a time and then accelerate and surpass them at another age. Again, we are faced with the problem of an unpredictable, mysterious, organic creature being held up to our crude measuring instruments and our unreliable sorting techniques.

Schools have tried all kinds of calibration systems over the centuries. Many names have been put forward as the inventor of the grading system, but they all originate around the same time, the late eighteenth century, the height of the Industrial Revolution. Mass production, efficiency, standardization — these were the key values of the age. They continue to have a profound influence on schools today. In fact, they have a profound influence on the lives of individuals. Career paths, income, social status, and self-concept can be directly related to marks. The one thing that marks do not always tell us is how intelligent a person is or what a person knows. Some of the smartest students I have worked with have had low marks. Some of the most "simple-minded" have been at the top of the class. I intentionally use the word simple-minded to contrast them with the complex-minded student. Some students are very good at getting marks, but they don't always have very complex thoughts. Sometimes they are just very good at regurgitation.

Anyone who has ever been evaluated (which includes almost everyone) knows that evaluation is a highly subjective business. There is huge variability among evaluators. If the same assignment was to be marked by a group of people, we can be relatively sure there would be a broad range of marks. The fact that we still place so much blind faith in marks is testimony to our capacity for doublethink: "The power of holding two contradictory beliefs in one's mind simultaneously, and accepting both of them." Marks don't tell you much. Marks mean a lot. The explosion in standardized testing attempts to get past the subjective nature of marking, but as we know, these are poor indicators of intelligence or ability. Many schools in the United States are leaning away from SAT scores toward more subjective forms of evaluation in deciding who gains entrance.

Marking means different things to different teachers. For some teachers, marking is about being a teacher. It is their message to themselves and to the world. "I'm a tough teacher. I have high standards." Papers from these teachers are peppered with negative, sometimes sarcastic comments. You see lots of exclamation marks. Marking becomes a form of self-expression and self-definition for the teacher. For other teachers, marking becomes a way of trying to make the student feel good. "I don't want to hurt your feelings. It's more important that you feel good about yourself than that I give you an honest response to this piece of work." These papers are covered with "good" and "excellent" and the occasional smiley face. Some would see the harsh approach as productive, realistic, and motivating. Others would call it sadistic and destructive. Some would call the soft approach limp-wristed and pointless. Others would see it as constructive and affirming. So marking is not only highly subjective in the way it is done, but also in the way it is received.

How to Read Report Cards

We will not get rid of marks any time soon, but we could adopt a more enlightened approach about their significance. Marks are not the measure of a person. They are not even the measure of a person's intelligence. Parents can do a lot to help their children process or interpret their marks. When your child brings home a marked test, assignment, or report card, instead of proclaiming your judgement on it immediately, and thus defining the reality, ask your child "What do you think about your mark?" or "How do you feel about your mark?" It is so important to train a child to develop their own relationship with the systems of power that will influence their lives. We can teach them to passively accept these external judgements as truth, or we can help them to understand their limited nature.

The parent is such a powerful emotional force in a child's life. When parents come in with judgement and comments it can completely obliterate the child's perception of the situation. Whatever their response would have been to the evaluation is replaced by the response of the parent. The corollary of all this is that marks and evaluation become a double-edged sword: they become an experience of being judged by teachers *and* parents. Emotions run very high on the day report cards are given out at school, and the level of anxiety increases with each grade. "My mom's going to kill me!" "My dad will be so mad!" or "My mother is going to love this!" "I can't wait to show this to my dad!" These sentences reveal a profound truth that learning can turn into an exercise in pleasing parents. It becomes about approval or disapproval, acceptance or rejection. School comes to have an emotional power completely unrelated to learning.

If we were to let the child speak first and create their own response to marks, we might be surprised at some of the things they might say:

"I think I can do better."
"This mark doesn't really show my ability in that subject."
"This mark is low because the course is boring."
"This mark is low because the teacher doesn't make it interesting."
"This mark is high because the teacher is an easy marker."
"I'm really going to focus more on this course because that's the area
   I want to go into."

These comments usually represent the child's sincere and realistic thoughts about her marks. Of course, we should always be wary about blaming someone or something else for the quality of our performance, but sometimes it is true that external factors play a major role.

If we see a bad report card or a failing mark, our first response is to say, "Okay. Now it's time for me to get involved!" In my experience, no child wants to have low marks, and no child wants to fail. Again, the simple questions, "What do you think about your marks?" and "How do you feel about your marks?" can go a long way. We could also ask the child, "What do you think you need to do to raise your mark?," or even more simply, "What do you need?" If a student's marks are extremely low, we would do well to really listen to that child. Criticism, expressions of disappointment, or, worse, punishment, are not helpful responses. We need to teach problem-solving to our kids.

Step 1: Identify the problem(s) as specifically as possible.
Step 2: Choose one problem to work on.
Step 3: Brainstorm ways to solve this problem.
Step 4: Choose one of these ways to put into action.
Step 5: Put the solution into action.
Step 6: Monitor the results.
Step 7: If necessary, modify your approach based on the results.
Step 8: Go back to step 1 and start over.

Rather than taking control of the situation ourselves, we should help the child take control. There is a real opportunity here to learn. We only do harm when we turn it into a crisis. It becomes a problem *with* the child rather than a problem *for* the child. As I constantly remind anxious parents, your child's grade three report card will not be used to determine admission to university. When a parent becomes over-anxious about marks, this can simply increase the child's stress, which decreases the child's ability to function at an optimal level. The hand-wringing of the parent becomes an internal monologue for the child: "I'm stupid." "I can't do this." "I am a disappointment."

Even high-achieving students can suffer negative side effects from their marks. A common story students have related to me over the years goes as follows: "I bring home an excellent mark, say a 90 percent, and my mom or dad says, 'Where's the other 10 percent?'" Students always tell this story with frustration and anger. The underlying message is that nothing is ever good enough. That is part of the problem with our 100 percent scale. It implies a standard of perfection that very few, if any, can ever measure up to. It implies that perfection is possible, but not for you. The comment also points to the glass half-empty attitude toward life. Instead of marks being about what one has achieved, they can just as easily be seen as indicators of what one has not achieved, and this can be discouraging. "Where's the other 10 percent" may be intended as a motivator, but it is felt as a criticism.

Incentives or Bribes?

Another approach that some parents take with marks is the offering of rewards for good marks. We can apply the negative term "bribes" or the positive term "incentives." This strategy can work, but there are two dangers. The first one is setting the goal so unreasonably high that there is little chance of winning the reward. Instead of offering a reward for every A when the student has been consistently receiving Bs and Cs, one might offer a reward for every B, the goal being to get rid of the Cs. Or a reward might be offered for increasing one's overall average by 5 percent. Some kids respond very well to incentives and rewards. Many salespeople are motivated by the prospect of a commission or bonus, so why not kids? The reward can take the form of money, a gift, or a special activity. The downside of this approach is that it shifts the focus from learning for its own sake to the material reward. Students become extrinsically motivated instead of intrinsically motivated. What will the child do when there are no rewards? Just as we want to teach our children that virtue is its own reward, we want to teach them that learning is its own reward. We would never think to offer a child rewards or incentives for being kind and friendly. I think this approach should be used sparingly and only in certain cases. Alfie Kohn has written a whole book on the problems with this approach called *Punished by Rewards: The Trouble with Gold Stars, Incentive Plans, A's, Praise, and Other Bribes*. On the other hand, things like the Olympic Games, the stock market, and most of the world's major religions have capitalized on this approach. You decide.

How to Talk to Kids about Their Marks

I am a firm believer in talking to kids openly and honestly about all the issues raised in this book, especially this issue of marks: what they mean, what they do not mean, and their less-than-reliable nature. I think it is very important to talk to kids about the developmental timeline issue as it relates to evaluation. "You are being evaluated at a particular moment in time, but everyone develops on a different timeline. You might just not be there yet. You will get it eventually." A common and easily seen example would be something as simple as forming one's letters properly, getting your lowercase Bs and Ds to face the right way. I don't think I've ever seen a teenager get this wrong — they got it eventually. This conversation should happen especially with boys whose language development is different from girls. Notice I do not say "slower" than girls or that boys are "behind" girls in their development. There is simply a difference, generally speaking, between the cognitive development of boys and girls, particularly in the area of language. In broad general terms, boys' brains develop spatial functions like math and gross motor movement sooner than girls do. Girls' brains develop logical-linear functions and fine motor ability sooner than boys. When a boy's reading and writing are not at the same level as the girls in his primary level classes, we can say to the boy, "That is perfectly normal. That is what we would expect."

When we talk about marks, we are in the area of performance-based esteem, feeling good about yourself because of your demonstrated ability. This is a very healthy thing and we all need it. The problem arises when this is our main source of self-esteem. You are only as good as your last report card. You are only as good as your last goal in hockey. We always have to balance performance-based praise with unconditional positive regard, or to use a simpler word, love. We love our children not for what they *do*, we love them for who they *are*. As adults we forget this sometimes, especially if we spend our days in a work environment where we always have to prove ourselves. We know what kind of stress that creates and how it fails to feed the soul. We need to make sure that this same kind of atmosphere is not created at home where one is judged on their performance. Parents should always be wary when drawing analogies between the workplace and the home. "I don't like my job, but I get up and go every day." Is this a positive life lesson? That one is destined to live in a state of constant frustration and dissatisfaction? "My job is to get up and go to work every day. Your job right now is going to school." Yes, but you get paid; the child does not, and you can't buy anything with marks.

What Does it Mean to be Smart?

The idea of multiple intelligences has been well-documented. We even do a good job now in schools of teaching this concept to students and getting them to be aware of their own learning styles. "Differentiated instruction" is a current topic in education that is receiving much attention. The term refers to the designing of instructional methods that suit a broad range of learning styles. In spite of all these efforts, there are still several skills that predominate in schools and end up being the main criteria by which success is measured.

1. The two languages one must be proficient at in school are the language of words and the language of numbers: reading, writing, and math.

2. The cognitive function that is a prerequisite for academic success is memory. While great efforts have been made to emphasize the *application* of knowledge, *recall* is still essential.

3. The third characteristic of the "smart" student is perhaps the most problematic. It is the ability to focus on things one finds boring. Mel Levine calls it our "Attention Control System." In my experience, most children are capable of intense focus for long periods of time (even those diagnosed with Attention Deficit Disorder), but not all of these children do well in school. The reason is they are only willing to focus on things they find interesting. The main job of education for the past fifty or sixty years (since the invention of television) has been trying to make things interesting. We call it motivating the student, engaging the reluctant learner, or, to use simpler terms, making it fun. This raises an interesting question: does the "intrigue" of something lie in the thing itself or in the person who finds it interesting? I have a fairly broad range of interests, but there are some things I don't think I will ever find interesting. The funny thing about school is we expect everybody to be interested in everything!

Our concepts of intelligence are socially constructed, and nowhere are they constructed more strictly than at school. Intelligence could also be seen as situational. What it means to be "smart" at school may get you nowhere in other contexts. MBA programs are finding that high entrance marks are no indicator of success in the program and certainly no indicator of success in business. Many specialized programs now look at marks as only one part of the application process. Evidence of ability in any number of skill areas now take the form of portfolios, auditions, interviews, references, and other demonstrations of past performance or future potential. This transition to a more holistic and person-centred evaluation is a good thing and is evidence of the limited amount of information that marks provide.

9

What Has Changed Since You Went to School?

Reading is the New Latin

There was a time when Latin was offered in most high schools. It was seen as a basis for the study of romance languages and helpful for the study of law or medicine. The study of Latin began to die out around the same time as the rise of television. It was called a "dead language" and was no longer seen to have any relevance for students. It was not something you could use — and usefulness increasingly became the yardstick by which the value of anything done in school could be measured.

Today, it is the value of reading that is being questioned, not by educators or parents, but by students themselves. They are not just questioning it theoretically, they are actively disengaging from it. This is particularly true of reading anything long, like novels. No one would argue that basic literacy is an essential life skill. One needs to be able to decode the prompts on an ATM and the headings of various YouTube videos, but the practice of the sustained reading of many pages of text is quickly becoming obsolete, like Latin.

Scholars tell us that silent reading was not the norm until the late middle ages. Before that people read out loud to others. St. Augustine expressed surprise at seeing St. Ambrose reading silently, and the fact that St. Thomas Aquinas was able to read silently and retain what he had read was seen as miraculous by some. We are returning to a world where the sight of someone reading silently will be very rare. What will be even more rare will be the sight of someone reading for a sustained period of time.

We have entered the three-minute world. Anything that takes longer than three minutes is not worth our time. This is the new attention span. Not just for kids and teenagers who we like to point the finger at, but for adults as well. I speak across the country to conferences and parent groups, and my talks last anywhere from one hour to ninety minutes. I have been asked many times if I am on YouTube. I have been told many times that I should be — that this is the way to reach the largest audience. I have also been recommended to give a TED Talk, another example of the new bite-sized attention span. As the TED Blog recently advertised, "Only have three minutes for a video snack? You can now find TED Talks by length: 3, 6, 9, 12 or the classic 18-minutes." If the idea of listening to a speaker for an extended period of time is dying, imagine what is happening to the idea of reading for an extended period of time.

The length of the material students are required to read in school increases at precisely the same time their use of screens begins to increase. By grade seven or eight, the curriculum begins to include novel study, and high school requires a significant amount of reading longer texts. If there is one recent change that stands out in student behaviour, it is the decline in the willingness to read for extended periods of time. The reason is simply the competition reading faces. Until the mid-1980s, the only competition school really had was television. We still lived in a world that supported print literacy. There was still a collective memory about the experiences reading offered and a collective agreement about its value. That consensus is quickly passing away. When a teacher hands out a novel today, the first question in every student's mind is "Is there a movie of this?" If not, the next stop is the Internet where websites like SparkNotes will provide short chapter-by-chapter summaries, commentaries, and analysis free of charge. These sites support themselves with the extensive advertising embedded within the summary articles (a good visual distraction from the boring text summary). Today reading literature means reading about literature. Teenagers do not read the book; they read what the book's about. The previous generation had novel study guides that went by various titles like Coles Notes, but even that was a kind of book that you had to go to a bookstore and buy. That world is quickly passing away.

The Post-Literate Age

As Marshall McLuhan famously said in the 1960s, we are now a post-literate society. Our culture has returned to a kind of medieval attitude toward print. Extended reading and writing is something small elite groups do. Secondary schools and universities are trying desperately to keep these activities at the centre of schooling, but even some of the most conservative ivy league schools have replaced listening to lectures and writing essays with field work, role-playing games, online discussion, and other forms of experiential, interactive "e-learning." Having a book published was once seen as the ultimate way of getting your message out to a wide audience. Today, a blogger can get millions of hits a day or a YouTube video can have millions of views. If a book sells five thousand copies in Canada it is considered a bestseller. The Kony 2012 video now stands at over 96 million views — a shocking statistic for a thirty-minute video!

The world of print is not returning any time soon. While students from the 1950s to the 1980s only had to turn off the TV, students today have many more things buzzing, whirring, and flashing, not only in their living rooms and bedrooms, but in their pockets and purses as well. The smartphone has brought cyberspace into the palm of one's hand, accessible anywhere at any time. The decision to be literate today is a bigger decision than it has ever been before. The decision to be literate is the decision to immerse yourself in an older "operating system" — thousands of black symbols printed on a white background, moving the eye from left to right, and turning one page at a time in fixed sequential order. Who could imagine a less stimulating format? No pictures, no sound, and no choice. After reading page one, you have to go to page two. You have to follow a plot or the development of an idea over hundreds of pages. To the mind raised in cyberspace what could be more boring? In school, particularly high school, we see the canaries in the mine, and they are simply not reading — at least not any more than they absolutely have to.

The Dumbing Down of Literature

When we talk about reading literature, it can evoke a kind of nostalgia for a mythic past where everyone read thick novels. Did such a world ever exist? Would I like to return to such a world? Personally, that would be great.

I love to read novels — but that's just me. Most of the hostile reaction to reducing the number of English classes comes from English teachers and people who love to read. Those people, as teenagers, would still be able to pursue their interest. It just wouldn't be required of everyone.

Our educational system is based on the myth that whatever we want society to be, we just need to "program" it into our schools. This is no longer possible in an age where our programming comes more from media than it does from school. As Neil Postman said, school has become the second curriculum and media is the first curriculum.

We once believed that a liberal arts curriculum that included study of the great works of classic literature would immunize youth from the trivializing influence of popular culture and mass media. That trivial culture has now become the dominant culture — created by Viacom, CBS, Time Warner, News Corp, Bertelsmann, Sony, NBC Universal, Vivendi, Televisa, and The Walt Disney Company — the ten largest media conglomerates in the world. Shakespeare, Charles Dickens, and Jane Austen cannot fix it.

In most jurisdictions, literature is still being force fed to everyone. When your audience is everyone, the content of what you're doing and saying inevitably gets watered down so everyone can "get it." This is an insult to Shakespeare, Dickens, and Austen. The problem with English literature is that it can be watered down. You can turn *Romeo and Juliet* into a graphic novel of twenty pages. You can reduce *Great Expectations* to a word search. The great literary critic Harold Bloom, in his monumental work *The Western Canon*, lamented the demise of the study of the great classics in schools. Talking about Shakespeare's *Julius Caesar*, he said, "Teachers now tell me of many schools where the play can no longer be read through, since students find it beyond their attention spans. In two places reported to me, the making of cardboard shields and swords has replaced the reading and discussion of the play." This is absolutely true, and the most tragic part of this scene is that there are kids sitting in that classroom who are very capable of a close reading of the Shakespearean text, kids whose lives and minds would be hugely enriched by such reading. Because the bar has been lowered so that everyone can jump over it, they may never experience the complexity and sophistication of Shakespeare. Some schools have taken to reading graphic novels of his plays; others will read famous passages. I lament this loss not for those students who have no desire or aptitude for this kind of study, but for those students who do. They are missing something. This is what happens when you require everyone, regardless of their interests or aptitude, to study great literature. The maths and sciences are faring better when it comes to maintaining academic standards firstly because it is much harder to water down algebra, calculus, chemistry, or physics, and secondly, we do not require everyone to take these courses.

One method of stemming the tide of watering down learning has been the addition of other academic levels: the International Baccalaureate and Advanced Placement programs. These programs are internationally recognized, the curriculum is externally developed and monitored and evaluations are also done externally. They are seen as a kind of guarantee or "gold standard" for consumers of education — students, parents, and post-secondary institutions. Their proliferation is testimony to what has changed in high schools.

The Need for Earlier Specialization

School and its processes are the product of a print-based culture, and nothing is more highly prized and rewarded than the ability to process text. "But I'm going to be a video game designer!" protests one of my grade ten English students. "I don't need to be able to read novels or write essays to do that." The way the game is rigged right now, in order to gain admission to a reputable video-game design program in a traditional post-secondary institution, one must have a high overall average coming out of high school, with a high mark in English — still the one grade twelve credit that almost all post-secondary programs require. In order to do well in grade twelve English, you must be proficient at reading extended texts and writing extended essays. The fact that you may already be able to design a video game or that you are a genius with computers will not help you if you do not have the stickers the institution is giving out.

What is to be done for this future video game designer who has to jump over the hurdle of grade twelve English before he can do what he is good at? By grade twelve a student should know what general area they would like to concentrate on. If they don't know it's generally because they've been so busy doing a little bit of everything and they haven't been able to develop proficiency in one area. Schools should not require such general proficiency so late in the life of a child. They should be able to specialize earlier. I worked with a student who was a great artist, but had difficulty with reading and writing that kept him from getting the kinds of grades he needed to enter a fine arts program. He wanted to be an art teacher, and would have made an excellent one, but the way was barred because of his weaknesses in reading and writing. Many students who are proficient in one area are not able to focus on that ability. They are distracted by all the other requirements of school in which they have no interest at all, and they become discouraged by their lack of success in those areas. If the young computer whiz, creative writer, machine tinkerer, actor, chef, or hair dresser was able to throw him or herself into their passion at a younger age, they would achieve far more and be happier. The study of English literature, currently required of everyone, should become one among many options.

Elective courses stand a better chance than mandatory ones. These courses are chosen by students with a genuine interest. The key words are "chosen" and "interest." As soon as you have these two things present — freedom and genuine interest — something incredible can happen in the classroom. The school of the future will have to allow more of this kind of choice. The study of great literature should work on the law of attraction not the law of compulsion.

New Attitudes Toward Authority

"I'm not going to do this and you can't make me!"

In the twentieth century our culture underwent a radical transformation in its attitudes toward authority. The 1960s were a time of rebellion against structures of power rooted in a perception of abuse of power. The Vietnam War was the catalyst for a loss of faith in the people in charge and the decisions they were making. In the following decade it was the Watergate scandal that reinforced our distrust of authority figures. When the president of the United States was seen to be involved in illegal activities and attempts to cover them up, our respect for politicians declined and we entered a new era of cynicism.

By the 1990s the Internet became a pervasive social force that transformed our attitudes toward authority even more. As Marshal McLuhan illustrated, the media we use has a huge effect on the way we think. When he famously wrote "the medium is the message," he had no experience of the Internet. This medium contains a message that is radically transforming our society. We grew up in a top-down, hierarchical world. The metaphor for all our social structures has been the pyramid — that Masonic symbol from ancient times that even found its way onto the back of the American dollar bill. The pyramid in the image is crowned by an all-seeing eye, perhaps representing an omniscient god, but the message of the icon is clear. Power resides at the top with the few and trickles down to the many. The stability of society depends upon the maintenance of this structure — the many must obey the few. Those in charge are not to be questioned. We grew up in a world where the answer to "Why should I do this?" was "Because I said so," and that was a good enough answer.

If the central social metaphor for previous generations was the pyramid, the central social metaphor for the current generation is the web — a complex array of social connections. The direction is not top-down, but every which way. In the pyramid metaphor, there was really only one direction of power — from the top down. In the web metaphor, the directions of power are much more complex. Perhaps an even better description of our current environment can be found in the word *Inter*-net. There are many nets and they are all inter-connected. This metaphor takes us away from the idea of a centre of power and control and implies a much more chaotic and random series of social connections with many centres.

If major corporations like Google continue to dominate the Internet, it may end up resembling a centralized web, and the all-seeing eye at the top of the pyramid will be replaced with the all-consuming spider in the middle of the web. This would be unfortunate. The Internet offers us the possibility of a radical kind of democracy. To have it controlled by one or several corporations would be a return to autocracy.

Right now no one controls the web. It has no head office. If you don't like what's there, there is no one you can complain to. On the Internet, you can say and do pretty much anything you want. It is a radically democratic medium where everyone can have a voice. The touch screen, the keyboard, the mouse, and the controller make it a completely interactive medium. Because television required passive observation, it didn't really pose the threat to education that everyone thought it would. One's passive observation skills could be transferred to school. It just meant that school had to become more entertaining, which it tried to do, with varying degrees of success. But when one comes to school from an interactive environment that is predicated upon choice into an environment that is predicated upon passive submission to authority, one has a problem.

The school of the future will have to allow students much more autonomy and choice. Teachers will need to realize that their authority in the classroom is not an automatic by-product of the role they play. We have lost our faith in roles because so many roles have been abused. Young people today reply much more strongly to things like personal integrity, kindness, fairness, subject-related expertise, and pedagogical skill than ever before. In short, if you want a student's respect today, you have to *earn* it — and this is not such a bad development. Many teachers survive in a profession they are not suited for because they are protected by the role they play. Students see this and are much more likely to respond by withdrawing respect and compliance. Today's students are more sophisticated consumers than we ever were. "Because I said so" does not have the power it once did, and that is a good thing because many of the things we were commanded to do were pointless at best and harmful at worst.

Freedom Teaches Responsibility

When it comes to children, we are still very conflicted about who is in charge and where the boundaries lie between being too controlling and too permissive. The media jumps on stories about six-year-olds walking to school alone in New York City precisely because it touches this nerve. We teach responsibility through freedom. The trick is to know how much freedom and how early. It is the parent's legitimate role to assess the risks involved in a situation and decide on the level of freedom, but risk-assessment is something we must also teach our kids from as early an age as possible, and we have to trust their judgement and allow them to make mistakes. If they make a poor assessment of the risk, our tendency is to veto their decision. Sometimes the better response is to let natural consequences play out so that the child can learn the important relationship between decisions and consequences.

I see so many children who are incapable of making good decisions for the simple reason that they have had so little practice at it. And that practice has to begin at an early age. Those low-level "bad choices" at age ten, like not doing your homework or not wearing your boots or spending all your money on the new video game, turn into much bigger bad choices in adolescence: drug use, skipping class, driving under the influence. The child who is always sheltered from the negative effects of his own choices or who is simply not allowed to make simple choices will be ill-prepared for the bigger choices of adolescence when Mom and Dad are not there to shelter or veto. Ultimately, we need to become the masters of our own destiny, the authors of our own scripts. We are not raising children, we are raising adults. A good teacher focusses on outcomes. What do they want the child to learn? One begins with the end in mind. We need to adopt the same approach with children. What do we want the end result of our child-rearing practices to be? We want a strong, confident, self-directing adult. We do not want to raise young people who cannot stand on their own two feet, who live according to the maxim "What would my mother do?" or "What would my parents approve of?" Sadly, I see so many young people who don't know what to do when there is no one there to tell them.

Worse than this, their definition of freedom becomes doing something that Mom or Dad or the teacher would never allow. Freedom becomes associated with anti-social behaviour. Doing things that no authority figure (parents, teachers, police) would approve of becomes the ultimate expression of freedom and autonomy. A lot of anti-social behaviour among the young, like hooliganism, gang violence, or simple acts of breaking the law like shoplifting and speeding are often an assertion of the self by people who have not had enough opportunities for self-assertion or self-expression. People who act in destructive ways often do so because they feel powerless. People who have a strong sense of personal power do not feel the need to gain more of it in anti-social ways.

This dynamic can be found every day in high schools. We see constant low-level attempts to assert autonomy in negative ways, from wearing the forbidden baseball cap in the hallways, to disrupting the classroom, to graffiti on the walls. All of these behaviours are symptomatic of our failure to instill in kids a strong sense of personal power. In fact, we often label "a strong sense of personal power" as "a sense of entitlement" or, worse, being "spoiled." We look with disdain at the child who speaks up for himself and questions the arbitrary dictates of the authority figure. In an environment where children are listened to respectfully and authentically, *no matter what they say*, there will be much less anti-social behaviour or acting out. When kids are acting out, our job is to pay attention. "You're not the boss of me!" means "I want to take ownership for my own actions." We interpret it negatively to mean, "I want to do whatever I want." Instead of seeing it as a positive declaration of independence, we see it as spoiled, irresponsible, and self-centred. We also see it as a threat to our own power and control. If we are raising young adults who we want to take control of their own lives, then we must inevitably relinquish our own control over them.

In school we are not doing enough to teach kids to take responsibility for their own actions. We are teaching them to obey authority unquestioningly. We teach them to hand over their sense of personal responsibility for themselves to the institution. I approached a school bus recently facing me in the opposite lane with its lights flashing. A little girl around ten years old got off the bus and ran around the front of it and across my lane of traffic. She didn't look up or left or right. My car was at a distance but still moving. She seemed oblivious to her external situation. I think this scene exemplifies the way we learn at a very early age to let systems and authority figures do our thinking for us. This little girl was operating under the unconscious assumption that larger forces were protecting her. She did not have to take personal responsibility for her own safety. The natural response of looking out for herself had been trained out of her.

Parents and schools need to do a better job of explicitly teaching kids to assess the risks in a particular situation and take responsibility for their own decisions. All too often this teaching takes the form of punishment after a bad decision has been made. It ends up being more about guilt and shame than teaching. "What were you thinking?" gets heard as "How could you be so stupid?" We need to anticipate situations where children and adolescents will have to make difficult choices and explicitly guide them through the kinds of decision-making processes they will need to practice on their own.

At School We Learn How to Follow the Crowd

At school, personal responsibility can also get lost in the group. Psychologists tell us the larger the group we are in, the less sense of personal responsibility we feel. A classroom can be a group of twenty-five to thirty kids. A school yard contains hundreds. We will say and do things in a group that we would never say or do on our own. When I was in grade ten, our class was assigned a teacher who did not speak English very well and was extremely insecure in his role. The class harassed him mercilessly, and I cringe to remember how I sometimes joined in the abuse, if only by laughing and thereby encouraging the more verbal bullies. He was obviously a very kind and sensitive man, and I was surprised and ashamed to see myself behaving in a way I would never have behaved towards him one-on-one or even in a smaller group. It was a powerful lesson for me in the power of the mindless mob. My sense of individual responsibility for my own behaviour was subsumed by the behaviour of the group. This phenomenon is quite common at school. Our individual freedom becomes absorbed by the "choices" of the group and the rituals of the institution.

When I teach *To Kill a Mockingbird*, I make this a specific lesson. In one scene, a lynch mob comes to take Tom Robinson, a black man who has been wrongly accused of raping a white girl. Atticus Finch, his lawyer, stationed himself outside the small-town jail to ward off the mob. Things were not going well until Scout, Atticus's nine-year-old daughter, rushes into the middle of the mob to be near her father. With tensions running high, Scout recognizes one of the men as the father of a boy she goes to school with. "Hey Mr. Cunningham … Don't you remember me…? I go to school with Walter." Speaking as an individual, she attempts a dialogue with him as an individual, and thereby breaks the spell of the mob. Mr. Cunningham is transformed from anonymous mob member to the father he truly is. There is a long, awkward silence, and then, "I'll tell him you said hey, little lady…. Let's clear out. Let's get going, boys," and the mob disperses.

The scene always makes an impression on my grade nine students because by this age they have all felt the power of the mob — sometimes as members of one and sometimes as the victims of one. I talk to them about the way mobs can make us do things we would never do on our own. I talk about the importance of never letting the mob rob you of your free will. This scene, indeed the whole book, is about the power of the individual.

Kids need to be taught this lesson, perhaps now more than ever. In school mobs are pervasive; in fact, the whole school itself can be seen as a kind of mob. Both kids and teachers need to be aware that sometimes we are operating as individuals and sometimes we get drawn into the unconsciousness of the institutional mob where we say and do — and even think — things that are not us. We tell kids not to follow the crowd, and yet that's what school is sometimes — a crowd we follow without questioning.

There are students in our schools who refuse to follow the crowd. Sometimes this individuality takes a positive form, sometimes it takes an anti-social or non-compliant form. We would do well to pay attention to both types of students. We see the bright, articulate leaders who are not interested in fitting in or being cool. The other kids respect them because of their independent attitude. These kids are very nice to have in the classroom. They offer fresh perspectives and model confidence and autonomy. But, of course, the nicest thing about them is that they don't rock the boat. These kids have learned how to maintain their unique perspective while operating within the confines of the machinery of school. They do not feel the limitations of the institution as a constraint. They are willing to play the game. They see the payoff available to them, and the ends justify the means. If they have to conform to these constraints for a couple of hours or days or months or years, they're willing to pay that price.

There are other students in our schools whose refusal to follow the crowd takes on negative forms. These are the non-compliant, so-called "bad" kids — the rebels or black sheep. We find them in the principal's office, the detention room, the smoking area, or at home because they're skipping. These kids are sometimes lone wolves; sometimes they form their own sub-culture and become crowd-followers of a different sort.

Both of these kinds of kids have something to teach us, because they both expose the power of the mob that is school. What are we doing to satisfy the needs of the strong, confident, independent thinker? Do we listen to this student's ideas? Is this student given leadership roles in the school, or do we see him or her as a threat to the status quo? For many years a colleague and I have supervised a student council. We have tried to attract these independent-minded kids and have tried to give them a sense of empowerment — a voice within the institution. We have tried to do this by leaving them alone and letting them say what they have to say. The trick is creating an atmosphere of freedom where students feel as though their voice is being listened to. The way we have accomplished this has been by backing off as far as possible. We set ourselves up in a completely advisory role. We attend all meetings, but we only speak when we are asked for advice on a matter. If we have a question or a suggestion, we raise our hands like the others and wait to be called upon. In student council, the students are in charge. This has been an attempt to create an experience of democracy in an otherwise totalitarian atmosphere. Unfortunately, some very bright, independent, and strong students have come to student council and seen within a few weeks that there are limits to the power and efficacy of the students within the school — that the real power lies in the front office. They perceive this attempt at democracy as lip service, and they stop coming. These are perhaps the most authentic and intelligent students and it's a shame to lose them, but their perceptions are accurate. There are real limits to students' power and students' voices. The school of the future is going to be a place where these students are listened to and included in the running of the school. We lose so much by not having them at the table!

And what about the "bad" kids, the rebels without causes? Schools especially need to listen to them. They stand as the most blatant judgement on what we are doing. If a society is to be judged by how it treats its weakest members, then we are judged by those students who feel alienated and displaced within the system. These students do not *choose* to stand outside the herd; their position is a *reaction* to something, a reaction that is many years in the making. I think most kids come into school with reasonably high hopes that it is going to work. They may be nervous and intimidated on first entry, but even they would admit that this is natural and the negative feelings will soon dissipate. For a number of kids, and I would suggest the number is growing, the feeling does not dissipate. School remains an *uncomfortable* place. The child perceives on a very visceral, unconscious level, that this just isn't working for them.

In Robertson Davies's great Canadian novel, *Fifth Business*, the child Paul Dempster finds himself in an abusive relationship with his guardian. He says, "I accepted it as all children accept the world created for them by adults." This is a chilling sentence, because it shows just how much power adults have because of the trust placed in them by children. What is even more chilling to me is the realization that sometimes this sacred trust is violated, and the world we create for children is not in their best interests or is not hospitable to their nature. The proof lies in the existence of kids for whom school is a daily torture, or, less dramatically, the kids who are slowly, imperceptibly ground down by school, so that the only way they can cope by high school is by getting away from it as much as possible — by skipping classes, hanging out in the smoking area, and turning to drugs and alcohol to numb the frustration.

The school of the future is going to have to face these kids and address their unmet needs. How can we change what we do in the earliest years, when this trajectory begins, to prevent it? How can we make the school fit this kind of child, since it is obvious that this kind of child is not willing or able to fit the school. In the past, we have seen this as a moral weakness on the part of the child. It is time to look at the moral culpability of the institution. Some of these kids are brilliant, some are incredibly creative, some are lovers, some are doers — who would do anything for something they believed in and were committed to. And all this human potential is being lost or squandered.

Our ADD Culture

"This is boring and I'm not going to do it!"

We live in a culture that has reduced all experiences into two categories: fun or boring. The greatest compliment a child can make about an experience is that it was fun. The worst judgement to be passed is that it was boring. As Neil Postman showed in his classic work *Amusing Ourselves to Death*, entertainment has become the paradigm for all experiences. Everything must be entertaining. This means it must not challenge us too much, stimulate as many of the senses as possible, and entail constant novelty. In other words, require as little focus as possible. To put it even more precisely, *it* must do the work of *attracting* my attention. I must not be required to consciously focus on it.

Our kids are growing up in this ADD culture — a culture based on the principle of distraction. We are constantly being asked to "look over here!" And when we look over there, there is another sound, flashing light, or picture saying, "Look over here!" All screen experiences are based on the principle of visual attraction.

The Triumph of the Screen

In the recent past, there was only one screen competing with school — the television. It could only be found in one room in the house and watching it was usually a shared family experience. Today, there are many different kinds of screens; they are found everywhere, can be carried anywhere, and are experienced alone. School has not become more boring, kids' expectations of what school should be have been changed by screens. The more time you spend on screens, the more boring school becomes. Screens are a spatial experience. School is a logical-linear verbal experience. Screens are a feast of looking and moving through space. School consists of a diet of reading, writing, listening, and speaking. Screen time is a solitary experience. When you are on a screen, it is always your turn. You never have to wait in line or raise your hand before you do something. When a child enters school, they enter a social world where there is a lot of turn-taking, waiting in lines, and raising of hands. There are many social interactions to be negotiated. When moving through cyberspace, especially in video games, you really feel like you're moving. Researchers have found that there are micro-movements in the muscles of the arms and legs of a gamer when their avatar is moving. Even if the child's body is not physically moving, he feels as though he is. Contrast this with sitting in a chair at a desk for hours at a time. The frustration can be excruciating! The child literally feels trapped. In cyberspace you are always in charge. The name of the device kids hold says it all — the "controller." When a child comes to school someone else is holding the controller. Someone else has the mouse. They want to minimize the screen, but they can't. The teacher just keeps talking and there's nothing they can do. On the screen, kids make all the decisions. In school, adults seem to be making all the decisions. On a screen you always get your own way. In school you don't. Conclusion: school sucks!

The reason for pointing out these contrasts is not to show how hopeless the situation is, nor to disparage kids for their love of screens. There are three reasons for pointing out the disconnect between cyberspace and school space:

1. The need for empathy. Our kids have a challenge we did not have. They did not create the technologies they love so much. Adults create them, promote them and provide them. Our ADD

screen culture is not the fault of kids. It is the air they breathe. And yet they are being asked to perform and produce in the print-base world of school. They need our understanding, not our lectures.

2. Kids need to realize the incredible leap they need to make in order to get the stickers school is handing out. There are currently very few rewards in the educational system for kids who are good with screens. That may change in the future, but the number one skill that is valued in every classroom today is the processing of text — reading and writing. That is the skill that will get you places, no matter where you want to go. Successful kids living in this time of transition will be those who are willing to do things they find boring. Kids need to be shown how the decision to be print literate is a bigger decision than it's ever been before.

3. As we move from a print-based culture to a visual-spatial culture, school is going to have to change. Reading textbooks and writing essays, tests, and exams are no longer valid methods of training for the worker of the future.

Here are ten abilities the person of the future will need to be successful. Not all, but some of these are actually learned better on a screen. The ability to:

1. interpret and synthesize a wide range of information (not one subject at a time);
2. communicate effectively through speaking (not just writing);
3. navigate complex information environments online (not just notebooks, binders, and textbooks);
4. think creatively (rather than just getting the right answer);
5. work independently (rather than under the watchful eye of a taskmaster-teacher);
6. show initiative (rather than obedience or compliance);
7. deal with continuous change (rather than routine and standardized procedures);
8. interact with a wide variety of cultures, roles, and norms (rather than homogeneous groupings, like "grade five");

9. manage their own physical and mental health (physical health is a school subject, mental health is not);
10. and form meaningful relationships (not superficial acquaintances as a result of close physical proximity).

As we re-design the school of the future, we must ask ourselves how we can achieve these goals and let go of our blind faith in those practices that actually mitigate against them.

No Touching!

Our culture has become very neurotic about touch. A neurosis is a psychic conflict. In this case, the conflict is between something we want and something we feel suspicious of, between something we need and something we fear. This is a recipe for craziness. Because we live in such a sexualized culture, all forms of touch have come to have a sexual association. It is a very sad state of affairs. Many people, especially children, have a strong need and desire for physical touch. It is calming and reassuring for them. Touch has been shown to promote mental health, physical health, and even cognitive functioning. Adults who work with children are particularly well-placed to satisfy this very natural and positive need in children.

In the last few decades, a chill has descended on adults who work with children. There is great fear on the part of care givers that one's touch will be misinterpreted. There is great fear on the part of parents that their child might be victimized. Of course, media has been the main influence in this chill. Detailed reporting of the most heinous cases of sexual abuse has led to an almost hysterical public response. Children are seldom alone, they don't play outside, and no adult is free of suspicion. The fragile fabric of trust has been torn by a handful of notorious criminals. Men have been the particular victims of this chill. Because most perpetrators are men, all men have become suspect. I read an interview with a hockey coach who said he always carries an umbrella in the trunk of his car in case a child has to wait for a ride after hockey practice. If it's raining, he will not sit in the car with the child. He will stand outside under his umbrella. Another hockey coach proclaimed his moral mantra with powerful conviction, "You *never* touch a child."

While caution is reasonable, and potential threats do exist, something very precious has been lost — human connection and nurturing behaviour. What positive conversation could have taken place in that car between the coach and the child? How many boys could benefit from a pat on the shoulder, head, or even, God forbid, a hug from the male figures in their lives? When we talk about something being inappropriate, we have to ask, inappropriate according to what yardstick or inappropriate to whom? Is the yardstick a moral one or simply based on current social norms? If the measure is a moral one, then what moral principle is violated by touch? If the measure is one of social convention, then how arbitrary and valid is the no-touch rule?

We have even seen the rise of the "no-touch school" — schools where no touching of any kind is permitted among the students. This is usually presented as an anti-bullying strategy, but the implications are much larger. The lesson taught is that touching is bad. It is a toxic teaching that will have negative outcomes. Children should be permitted to express their natural inclinations to hold hands, hug, and walk with arms around each other. These are positive and beautiful forms of touch. Adults should not be afraid to hold the hand of a child, to give a child a hug, or a rub on the back, arm, or head. Of course we need reasonable boundaries, but if we put ourselves and those around us in impregnable bubbles, these are not reasonable boundaries.

Sometimes it seems not so much that we fear adults molesting our kids, it's more that we fear them breaking the fear rule. This is something we are all supposed to be afraid of and we become afraid when someone is not afraid of it too. We all know that child sexual abuse exists, but when the hockey coach puts his arm around a boy's shoulder, he is not violating the boy, he is violating the fear rule. We have all decided that this is something we will be afraid of, even when we can see that it's actually a good thing.

It is also ironic that we limit touch to family members, when the statistics show that the majority of child sexual abuse is perpetrated by family members or friends of the family. It is always the mysterious "other" we need to be afraid of. It is an evil that lurks "out there." This is how we protect ourselves, oddly, from the truth. The worst part of all this is that we pass this fear on to our children. They become confused and fearful about touch

— a fundamental human need becomes distorted, deformed, and laden with associations it shouldn't have. Kids need to learn to interpret touch and to set their own boundaries. They can only learn this through experience. No-touch policies allow no opportunity to practice this. The teaching of "good touch, bad touch" is still the best policy for children.

We need to talk back to this boogie man we have created ourselves. We need to reclaim the value of nurturing touch. We need to be respectful of boundaries, but not neurotic about them. Many men avoid teaching as a profession because of the perceived risks. If a female teacher hugs a child, this is seen as positive. If a male teacher hugs a child, it is seen as suspicious. As one senior administrator said, it's all about optics. Who is looking and what judgement are they passing? This is the boogie man that needs to be talked back to. Men need to claim their role as kind, loving, and nurturing caregivers. We must also talk back to a culture that has made all touch sexual and lost the important connection between mind and body. We are our bodies, and we communicate profoundly through touch.

We Need More Male Teachers

Teaching is a predominantly female profession. We need more men in the classroom in all grades and subject areas. Children in the primary grades need to see men in a nurturing role who are capable of addressing the emotional needs of children as well as their academic needs. This foundational role-modelling is essential for children of both genders while they learn what it means to be male or female. They need to learn from their lived experience that men can be nurturing and caring.

We also need to have more men in the classroom if we are ever going to get more men to choose teaching as a career. Male teachers would show boys that working with children is a possible choice for their own gender. They learn this when they see men at the front of the classroom. In middle schools where kids are going through puberty, they need to have the opportunity to interact with both genders — a woman who is not their mother and a man who is not their father. Boys rely very much on role models at this stage. They are in a period of transition away from the mother as primary attachment figure and need to see positive male role models who present a picture of what's next for them in their development.

Girls too at this age need to see men who are strong, kind, and confident, men who will relate to them in positive, respectful, and nurturing ways. As children develop their sexual identities, all relationships — with their own gender as well as those with the opposite sex — form templates that will influence all future conceptions of gender and relationships. In high schools men are most commonly found as math and science teachers. Kids need to see men in non-traditional roles, teaching the arts and English for example. Both boys and girls need to see the range of human endeavour spanning both genders, rather than seeing it divided into male and female subject areas, grade levels, or professions.

School Shootings

In the aftermath of the Sandy Hook Elementary School shootings, we all woke up for a few days or weeks and spoke the truth. Then we all went back to sleep. We talked about gun violence, alienated youth, the various systems that did or did not respond to the situation, and how the tragedy might have been prevented.

As someone who has spent each working day in school for the past thirty years, I have always had one question: why schools? Since Columbine in 1999, "school shootings" has become a crime genre. If a gunman is looking for crowds, he could choose a mall, a church, or a movie theatre — and some have done so, but these have not become a distinct genre.

Gunmen choose schools, and school shootings have become a genre because schools embody a central contradiction that we have all experienced. In our collective imaginations, schools are safe havens. Schools are places where we will be loved, nurtured, and protected. In school we are all special and unique snowflakes. On the other hand, school is a place where we are subjected to pressure to perform and regular judgement on our performance. It is a place where special and unique snowflakes are required to conform to a mold. The problem lies in the fact that school is both of these things at the same time, and it makes for a very schizophrenic existence. Am I loved or am I hated? Am I succeeding or am I failing? Am I accepted or rejected? Do I stand out or do I fit in? School is one of the most confusing institutions we have ever devised.

Most of us can bear the contradictions. The teacher tells us what a good job we did one day and the next day we get a test back with 55 percent. We are told to be ourselves, and the next day we are sent to the office for inappropriate behaviour.

Add to this the fact that in school, students live in two separate worlds — learning world and kid world. Learning world is all about performance and marks and getting ahead. Kid world is all about social acceptance. The bottom line in both worlds is "fit in." Again, most of us endure and survive this tension.

I believe that many school shooters are trauma victims who return to the site of their trauma to try to resolve the huge internal conflict they feel about their experience in school. They are often the dispossessed, the alienated, and the outsiders. Most of us survive the trauma of school because we have other people — parents, siblings, and friends — who affirm us. A former classmate, remembering the shooter, Adam Lanza, to the *New York Times* said, "I never saw him with anyone. I can't even think of one person that was associated with him."

Asperger Syndrome has been mentioned in connection with the killer. It could well be the case — trouble with social interactions and a preference for routine behaviours make children with Aspergers ideal candidates for getting lost in school. They follow the three rules of school very well: sit still, be quiet, and do what you're told. In addition, I would guess that this boy's psychological profile would include high intelligence and extreme sensitivity — two characteristics that can make school a difficult place to be. Intelligence is not always recognized or rewarded at school. We hear that he got good marks, but this is not the same thing as being intellectually challenged or stimulated. And as for being highly sensitive, well, we just don't have time for that. Life is hard. You better get used to it.

Finally, these shooters are all boys. We have tried to blame video games, but that hasn't stuck. Testosterone is certainly a factor, and by the time a little boy is twenty years old, he has enough testosterone to fuel the anger that has been building for about fifteen years.

I would argue that it is no coincidence that school shooters are always boys. They are among the most traumatized at school. Whether it is because they are highly kinesthetic and therefore bored by all the sitting and reading and writing, or they're intelligent and not challenged by the curriculum, or they're highly sensitive and bullied (both by peers and the system itself), we have a huge population of disenfranchised, alienated, angry males in our schools for whom the system simply does not work. School shooters are the dramatic tip of an iceberg that we see every day in the classroom. Kids who need to be seen for who they really are, not for who we want them to be, who need to be listened to no matter what they say, and who need to be touched with nurturing affection.

10

The Emotional Lives of Teenagers

What Drug Use Can Teach Us about School and Parenting

One of the deepest and most important questions we have to ask ourselves about school is what are we doing to contribute to the pervasive use of drugs and alcohol among young people? Of course school is not the sole cause of the problem. Genetics, family life, and the culture play just as significant roles, but when we consider that young people spend more than a third of their waking hours in school, we have to ask ourselves what are we doing to contribute to the problem or what could we be doing to help the problem.

Drug Use as a Symptom

Alcoholism is often referred to as a disease. The problem with this language is the way it puts the focus on the craving for alcohol and the act of drinking. It also puts all of the attention on the addict and lets environmental factors off the hook. It deflects attention from the causes behind the craving and the behaviour.

I find it more helpful to think of substance abuse as a symptom of a larger, deeper problem. Gabor Maté talks about American soldiers who used cocaine to cope in Vietnam and when they came home were able to stop. Only a small percentage were "true addicts" who could not stop using upon their return. The situation was the problem, not the person and not the addiction in itself.

For some kids, school is their Vietnam, and they are simply trying to survive. The war metaphor may be an apt one. Many kids feel as though they are in a hostile environment surrounded by enemies. They feel under constant threat. They take solace in "comrades in arms" and will gladly use whatever is offered as a sedative for their pervasive anxiety.

For many students, grade nine is a new beginning. They come in full of hope that this year will be different. High school will be better than elementary or middle school. Within a few weeks, the same patterns begin to emerge: low marks, failure, reprimands from adults, cruelty from peers, hostility from parents. That feeling of hope is slowly replaced by feelings of rejection, self-loathing, confusion, and anger. But they make it through grade nine. Every day is new for the first year. Maybe it will get better. In grade ten, the calendar simply repeats and the student realizes that this is as good as it gets. It is in grade ten that we lose so many, and there are older students — "brothers in arms" — who stand ready to supply them with solutions to their problems. All behaviour is logical. When a fifteen-year-old turns to marijuana, alcohol, or harder drugs, he is simply trying to cope. It takes a courageous and enlightened adult population to be willing to look at the truth behind this logic. To really deal with it, we would have to question ourselves and our approaches, and so many adults are unwilling to do that. Adults take refuge in the explanation that the problem is the kid, not the system. The kid is making "bad choices." What about the choices we've made as adults that have contributed to this situation? Those questions never get asked. We label the teen who turns to drugs as a "bad" kid when really he is a hurting kid. We blame the victim.

Our schools should do more for the students for whom it does not work. We can see that it's not working. Their files fill up with suspension letters, their marks are perpetually low. If a child has a diagnosed learning disability then they qualify for special education services, and this can be a help. There are many students, however, whose issues are behavioural and emotional, who do not qualify for special education support. Instead they are disciplined. This is no solution at all. In fact, it only makes the problem worse. We take kids with low self-esteem and we degrade them further. Many of the kids who get into drugs and alcohol are those with serious learning issues (diagnosed or undiagnosed) and serious emotional and behavioural issues. Many kids with ADD/ADHD, for example, turn to marijuana to self-medicate. They end up being yelled at and suspended, and nothing is ever done about their underlying condition.

For the child struggling with addiction, we have zero tolerance for possession of drugs or alcohol on school property. The result is immediate suspension and police involvement. The child is sent home for days or weeks. These kids need help more than they need punishment. Their parents also need help knowing how to deal with their child. The parent's response is often just an echo of the school's — rejection, criticism, humiliation, abandonment. How many kids are kicked out of the house after they've been kicked out of school? What must it be like to be kicked out of the most important places in your life? What must it be like to be rejected by the most important people in your life?

Our approaches to children would be transformed if we practiced the simple art of empathy. Put yourself in the child's shoes. See the problem from their point of view. We tend to see these problems (drugs, alcohol, and anti-social behaviour) from the point of view of the system. The violation of rules and the disruption of institutional decorum are the first things we see and the first problem to be addressed. The hurting child comes third or fourth, if at all.

As soon as we see a child "going off the tracks," we need to take special care of that child, especially in the earliest years. They need extra care and attention, not rejection. We need people in our schools who have the time and the personality to work one-on-one with kids who are struggling. We need a more child-centred education system where students are loved and respected — especially those for whom it's not working. If they are constantly going off the tracks, then maybe we need to find (or invent) other kinds of tracks. This takes us back to the need for greater diversity of pathways and programs in our schools. One size does not fit all, and those kids who turn to drugs and alcohol are living, hurting proof of this.

Is Drug Use a Choice?

There are two other issues that taint our thinking about addiction. The first one is our tendency to approach addiction in terms of the will power of the addict. We talk about making bad choices as though the individual is a completely free agent. Philosophically speaking, that may be true.

We are all free. But in real life we are often operating under influences over which we have no control, and, more importantly, of which we are completely unaware. The two most obvious examples of this are genetic predisposition and stresses in the environment. When we fail to acknowledge the important role these two things play, addiction quickly becomes a question of moral weakness. Why can't you just say no? Why are you so weak? Why are you such a follower? Addiction is not a choice.

Alcoholics Anonymous refers to alcoholism as a disease. The word disease makes me think of all the other disorders, dysfunctions, and disabilities we have named in which we pathologize the way certain individuals are made. I like to speak in terms of "brain profile" or "chemical profile." It's just the way you're made. People who are prone to addiction have a particular brain and chemical profile that makes them susceptible to the use of artificial stimulants and relaxants. This is not a moral issue, nor is it a sickness. The problem comes when you have to function in a society that is not conducive to your nature and creates stresses that trigger negative responses. In addition, the potential addict is born into a culture that has normalized all kinds of negative ways of dealing with stress, a culture that does nothing to reduce stress. We have accepted the use of chemicals to alter mood as normal. Caffeine as a stimulant and alcohol as a relaxant are the two most obvious socially sanctioned chemicals. It should be no surprise to us when a stressed teen turns to chemicals to alter his or her mood. Some observers have concluded we live in an addictive culture where creating cravings and satisfying them instantly is in the very hard drive of consumer capitalism. If this is true, then how is addictive behaviour a choice? It is a cultural teaching.

You Should Be Ashamed of Yourself!

The other issue that taints our thinking about addiction is shame. Because we see it as a choice, we feel entitled to pass negative judgement on those who make that choice. We are ashamed of them. They are ashamed of themselves. The language we use with them is shaming language. "How could you do that?" "What were you thinking?"

There are two kinds of shame — warranted and unwarranted. If someone willfully harms another, shame could be considered a very healthy response. We regret what we have done. We are ashamed of our behaviour. Ideally, we would like to make amends. Unwarranted shame occurs around events over which we have no or limited control. Sexual feelings and fantasies are probably the most common and are historically the most pervasive sources of shame. We have little control over these things, especially in adolescence, and yet some people have been taught to feel great shame about them. Unwarranted shame can be one of the most toxic and corrosive forces in a person's psyche. Shame does not just come to rest on the particular deed or feeling or impulse; it comes to rest on one's whole self-concept. The child does not conclude, "I did a bad thing." The child concludes, "I *am* bad."

Drug Use as a Spiritual Practice

Many of the kids I have worked with over the years who struggle with addiction have what I would call a spiritual temperament. They are often very sensitive kids who are looking for meaning in their lives. This complex inner life is amplified by a strong emotional life. These kids have so much going on inside them. When you add all the things that are going on outside them, it can be too much. Someone said the modern person experiences as much in one day as a medieval peasant experienced in a lifetime. There is just too much going on for some kids to process. Add to this the fact that kids are growing up in a world where spirituality is seen as some kind of eccentric hobby, or, if it takes the form of organized religion, as a kind of cult where each sect requires you to check your critical consciousness at the door.

These spiritual kids find themselves adrift in a culture where the commonly accepted yardstick of value is a material one. Value and importance are given to things that are expensive, current, and popular — the code word for this is "cool." There is a cool version of everything; there is a cool way to act in any given situation. Our lives are spent trying to figure out what this is — this constantly moving target — and keep up with the latest thing. Steve Jobs called it "the next big thing." He became a billionaire by capitalizing on the rule of cool and being there to provide the masses with the next big thing. He once said, "People don't know what they want until you show it to them." When Steve Jobs died, his picture was everywhere.

Like a modern-day Gandhi, he was the dead messiah who had delivered us all from our mundane existences and given us a tablet not made of stone. Steve Jobs embodied in one person our three greatest gods: fame, fortune, and technology. For the spiritual kid, this is not enough. The soul is not fed by these gods.

This vacuum of meaning creates stress and depression. Kids feel a pain they can't name, a hollowness they don't know how to fill. In a culture that has accepted the use of chemicals to alter mood, it is only natural that they would turn to alcohol and marijuana to "manage" their pain. It is referred to as self-medication.

Are We Talking About Drug Use or Drug Abuse?

When talking to worried parents about drug use, I like to make a distinction between use and abuse. Not every teenager who uses drugs is abusing them. Most teenagers will use chemicals like cigarettes, alcohol, and marijuana at least once. For many this will never progress beyond a couple of times a year in very particular circumstances. If we break down the factors contributing to the use of these chemicals, it becomes less frightening. One of our most natural and positive characteristics as humans is curiosity. We wonder what particular experiences are like. This is a positive trait that leads naturally to experimentation. The adolescent who experiments with cigarettes, alcohol, and marijuana is, at first, simply satisfying his or her natural curiosity. What does it taste like? What does it feel like to be drunk or high? If we are honest with ourselves, and can see beyond our own fear, these are not irrational or even negative ways of thinking.

The Need to Appear Grown Up

The other factor that contributes to drug use is the way in which it is seen as a symbol of maturity. The logic is simple: smoking and drinking are something adults do. Kids want to be adults, or they want to appear like an adult, so they will achieve their goal by doing things that only adults are allowed to do. Adolescence is a time when many kids chafe at the idea of being children. They are so anxious to grow up and have the same rights and freedoms as adults. Smoking and drinking are perceived as a quick and easy way to achieve this even if their age makes it illegal.

Do we keep our children in a state of childhood for too long? Is their desire to appear more grown up rooted in a legitimate need to be treated more like adults? Is there more we could do as parents and teachers to give them the kind of adult freedoms (and responsibilities) they are seeking? I think if adolescents were treated more like adults, they wouldn't feel as strong a need to prove that they were mature to themselves and others through superficial and possibly destructive means like drugs and alcohol.

"It's Fun to Get in Trouble"

The illicit nature of chemical use is the other reason it attracts teens. There is something dangerous about going outside the boundaries. In adolescence, particularly for males, there is great emotional power to be had from transgressing social boundaries. The "bad boy" image persists. Evolutionary biologists have suggested that risk-taking males who show a tendency or willingness to transgress boundaries are more desirable to females. It is a mark of status in the group. The James Dean rebel without a cause is alive and well. Some teens are natural risk-takers. They get a kind of "high" just from pushing the boundaries, but also from getting in trouble once caught. I have had students say to me with a sheepish grin, "It's fun to get in trouble."

Psychologists have identified something called reward deficiency syndrome, a brain chemistry profile that requires a greater stimulus for dopamine and endorphin production. For many people, a beautiful sunset or the anticipation of a birthday party can provide hours or days of positive feeling. For others, more powerful forms of stimulation are required in order to get the "feel good" chemicals flowing. If we have such a child, we need to be aware that they may be more susceptible to high-risk behaviour, and we might need to guide them to find those "feel good" experiences in socially sanctioned ways. Mountain biking, skateboarding, paintballing, lacrosse, and snowboarding are the kinds of activities that spring to mind. This can be a challenge for parents who cannot identify with this need at all. They see these high-risk activities as simply dangerous or wreckless. We can spot this reward deficiency syndrome in kids who are constantly *creating* high-risk situations in whatever environment they find themselves. Pushing and shoving in line, climbing up on the desk, hiding from adults who are looking for them. Is this child seeking stimulation? Our first response is to call the behaviour bad or to say the child is making bad choices. Sometimes the child is trying to satisfy a chemical need. In adolescence, these children may be susceptible to chemical or behaviour addictions if the need is not channelled in a positive direction.

The Need for Rebellion

Another factor in chemical use is rebellion as a form of self-definition. To smoke and drink is to rebel against the adults who have forbidden this activity since earliest childhood memory, mainly parents and teachers. In adolescence, the central project of life is to break away from childhood identity, which is largely associated with parents and everything they approved of, and establish a distinct, independent, adult identity. One logical way to accomplish this is by doing things which Mom and Dad would not approve of. When we engage in these kinds of behaviour, we are asserting an independent self. This could be seen as a very positive phenomenon. We do not want our children to stay in an eternal state of childhood, always trying to please Mommy and Daddy and simply accepting all of our values uncritically. We want our children to establish independent identities that may or may not include the behaviours and value systems we hold dear. When they experiment with drugs and alcohol, this kind of low-level rebellion as self-definition may be taking place.

When a Kid Goes "Off the Tracks"

It is natural to hope that your children will adopt the same core values as you hold. When they rebel in the teenage years we often feel they have abandoned everything we taught them. In my experience of seeing thousands of children pass through the teenage years into adulthood, I have been surprised and inspired by one simple fact. The deep core values held by a parent and passed on to the child, either implicitly or explicitly, *do* persist. In adulthood, their external circumstances may differ from what you had planned for them, but these are window dressing. The deep core values do persist. You coached them to speak up and assert themselves in social situations, and they end up as shy, reserved adults. You signed them up for every sport, and in adulthood they show no interest in sports. You taught them to value reading, you took them to the art gallery and the museum, and in adulthood they show no interest. These behaviours are better described as lifestyle choices. They have nothing to do with core values. Did you teach the child to respect him or herself, to respect others and be tolerant of differences? Did you teach your child that he is strong and confident and will be able to meet any obstacle in life with fortitude? Did you teach your children basic kindness to others? These are the kind of deep core values that get passed on and persist over time. They are not taught by precept. They are taught by example. I have worked with many teenagers who have "gone off the tracks" in adolescence, and I have stayed connected with them long enough to see what happens in adulthood. What I see is the persistence of the early childhood foundation — for good as well as for bad. Parents who have laid a strong core foundation of self-esteem in the earliest years will see that foundation re-emerge after the stormy years of adolescence. Kids who did not get a strong foundation will sometimes limp along for the rest of their lives. Some will create their own foundation. Some will partner with someone who has a stronger foundation and will benefit from that. Some will meet a mentor figure who will guide them in the creation of a foundation that lies unfinished or latent within them. As parents, the key is to have a set of strong positive core beliefs yourself. They will inevitably get passed on and persist in your children.

Core Self-Esteem

There are two kinds of self-esteem: performance-based esteem and core self-esteem. Performance-based esteem means you're as good as your last report card, your last goal in hockey, your last accomplishment. Esteem is something you earn through your performance, but what if you don't win? What if you don't even do well? For every gold star given out, how many kids are left with nothing? For many kids, not getting any gold stars becomes their normal. What does this do to one's self-esteem? Performance-based esteem is conditional.

Core self-esteem refers to the way you feel about yourself all the time, your baseline sense of yourself apart from those thrilling moments of accomplishment when one glows with pride. Our core self-esteem is far more important. How is it instilled, developed, and nurtured? First of all, core self-esteem is instilled through unconditional love. I love you for who you *are*, not for what you *do*. This can be a hard one for parents who were raised on conditional love. The unspoken messages included things like: "I'll love you if you behave in ways I like, if you act out the script I have planned for you, or you think the same way I do." Since these lines are never spoken out loud, they can be hard to identify in the present or recall from the past. We are raised with many unspoken rules and we end up living by many unspoken rules.

Core self-esteem has three ingredients: to be seen, to be listened to, and to be touched. If a child gets these three things in abundance, he or she will grow up to have strong core self-esteem. I say in abundance because sometimes we practice what can only be called sadistic with-holding. We know the child craves or needs something, and we don't give it. Whenever we behave in ways that are not indicative of our best nature, there is usually some fear lurking. The fear that lurks behind emotional withholding is that we could somehow spoil our child, make them "soft" or self-centered. The three needs listed above are sometimes referred to as narcissistic needs. They are not only natural for babies, infants, and children, they are essential to their development. If our narcissistic needs are met in childhood, we are more likely to grow up to be strong, confident adults who are capable of loving others and feeding the narcissistic needs of our own children. Many of the kids I see who turn to drugs and alcohol in adolescence are kids whose narcissistic needs were not met. They are still searching for those three things: to be seen, to be listened to, and to be touched.

The Need to Be Seen: Mirroring

"Mommy, look!" "Daddy, watch!" From a very young age, children are constantly bringing us things to show us, or doing things they want us to watch. The need to be looked at, the need to be seen, is one of the deepest needs we have. When the baby emerges from the mother's womb, researchers in attachment theory tell us that the first thing the baby looks for is the mother's eyes. When they meet, the baby relaxes. This is a safe place. There is someone here who will take care of them. They don't need to be afraid. As we move through the developmental stages, being looked at gives us our sense of identity. We know we exist because we have been seen by others. It is a profound existential phenomenon. It is called mirroring — a deep need we all have to see ourselves in the responses others have to us. What is deeply important is that the positive be mirrored back most. For many kids, especially as they get older, the negative gets mirrored back more than the positive. They begin to see themselves as "bad" because that's the dominant image of themselves being mirrored by the adults and peers around them. I had a boy in my grade nine class who had a history of impulsive, anti-social behaviour. He returned from a two-week suspension for a violent outburst. When he came back to school, there was fear in the faces of some of his teachers and classmates. He was seeing himself in a mirror, and the image he saw was: "I am someone to be feared or I am a person that others are afraid of. I am not a person that others love." Some other kids greeted him with bravado and gave him the high five — he was the warrior returned from battle. They were mirroring him as well. The image in the mirror said: "Being bad will get you the positive attention of some. That's better than nothing." What could we do in our schools to prevent these kinds of scripts from being played out? What could we do as teachers and parents to mirror the positive in our children more than the negative?

Peer Pressure

Why can't kids just say "no" when they're offered drugs and alcohol? Why do they always feel they have to go along with the crowd? We drive down our suburban street in mid-November and one of the neighbours has put up their Christmas lights. Our internal response is "Oh, it's time to put up our Christmas lights." The alpha-neighbours have decided it's time, and all the other homeowners on the street feel the pressure to conform. This may seem like a trivial anecdote and one that does not apply to all, but it speaks to a cultural tendency to place a very high value on conformity. It is not just kids who suffer from peer pressure; it has become a kind of habit that we all follow. Consumer capitalism depends upon it. We must compare what we have and do with what others have and do, and then we must copy them. This is how we gain social acceptance and how we assert our status in the social pecking order. The logos we wear, the make of car we drive, the vacations we take — the power of these social indicators is fuelled by peer pressure.

If we are honest with ourselves, the unwritten motto of many parents is "Don't stick out." Or to express it another way, "Fit in." We all want our children to fit in. We want to fit in ourselves. Evolutionary biologists tell us this is a survival trait, that there is protection in the herd, and rejection by the herd could mean death. That may have been true in prehistoric times, but today one wonders if following the herd is more dangerous than leaving the herd. Parents like to pose the rhetorical question, "If everyone jumped off a cliff, would you jump off too?" So many of our collective behaviours resemble jumping off a cliff. The need to choose alternative lifestyles seems more important than ever before. Do we model this kind of non-conformist behaviour for our kids? Do we show them that we are comfortable with being different? That it is okay not to have what everyone else has or do what everyone else does? This is such a hard one for parents, especially when kids reach early adolescence and the need for social acceptance increases, sometimes to a fever pitch. I am not suggesting that families need to live off the grid, but the decision to participate in collective values and behaviours should be a conscious one. It should not just be an automatic response. There should be discussion about the pros and cons of doing those things that everyone else is doing. We need to teach our kids to be free agents, not unconscious consumers. "Say no to drugs" just sounds hypocritical to a child raised in a family that says "yes" to everything that is deemed cool. When the cigarette is offered in grade seven or the joint is being passed around in grade ten, what is the default mechanism for that child? "Fit in by being cool" or "Make your own decisions about what the world offers you." From an early age we need to teach our children a sense of personal agency — you always have the freedom to choose. You must stay awake, weigh the pros and cons of your choices, and then make the choice that promotes life.

What We Could Learn From Kids' Music

Teenagers have more independent spirits than we give them credit for. Lots of kids listen to Top 40 pop music, but many listen to independent and obscure artists who have huge followings created by word-of-mouth. It has always amazed me how certain bands and singers become known to every young person but are never heard on mainstream radio stations. There is an underground communication network in youth culture that is not controlled by any corporation. It is controlled by the deep needs and loves of teenagers. Art has a life of its own that no corporation can control, and some kids are totally in touch with that powerful force. Music has become the central aesthetic experience for most young people and, I would suggest, the central spiritual practice. These songs are art, however primitive the form may be, and they provide an experience of transcendence in an otherwise materialistic culture. We only need to listen to the lyrics of the songs our kids our listening to to find out what their central concerns and core longings are. Of course, love and its loss are pervasive themes. The central project of adolescence is breaking from Mom and Dad as love objects and transferring one's affection to other loves. This can be a beautiful, pleasurable process or a tortuous one (usually it's both); hence, the ubiquitous love song. The other central project of adolescence is the establishment of an identity separate from the one constructed with Mom and Dad's help, or, perhaps more accurately, the one constructed by Mom and Dad. Many songs deal with the quest for identity and meaning in life and the trials involved in achieving this. We talk about "teenage angst" in a belittling way, but it is a very real thing and deserves our respect and attention. We could learn so much about young people by listening to the lyrics of the songs they love. Some are fatuous; some are profound.

Teen Tribalism: The New "Community"

The word "community" has been drained of its meaning. We have "Community Centres," one is encouraged to do "community service," the local media talks about things happening "in our community," school administrators talk about "our school community." For most young people, these words ring hollow. The word "community" has taken on a sterile, almost bureaucratic connotation. Communities are officially sanctioned, even promoted by the powers that be. There is something suspicious about the word community — an implied uniformity and conformity. One finds oneself in a community for reasons that are not always clear — accident of birth or accident of geographical location.

Young people form other communities that have a more primal quality. One might call them tribes. The difference between tribes and communities is that tribes are chosen. Teen tribes can be organized around common interests or activities such as music, gaming, smoking, or playing a particular sport. In each case, one of the things these kids get out of the tribe is a feeling of belonging, a feeling of connection — things that our communities once really did provide.

This need is even easier to satisfy with social networking. Kids can find people all over the world who share their interests. The Internet has been criticized for creating a kind of mirror in which we all see our own image reflected back. We only search those sites that reinforce our preconceived ideas, and we only communicate with those who see things the way we do. This is a danger, but it shows the absence of connection felt in the real world. Kids seek in tribes what they do not find in institutional settings like school.

The decentered school of the future will be less institutional, less of a "community," in the sterile sense of the word. It may take on a more tribal quality. One of the attractions of the TV series *Glee* was the depiction of a tribal school setting where the "drama types" formed a sub-culture where they could be themselves. We see something similar in the TV show *The Big Bang Theory*, where the geeks and nerds, while no longer in high school, form a kind of tribe where it's okay to be who they are. Sheldon's oddness becomes his most endearing quality. We can all imagine what life would have been like for Sheldon in the factory high school under the "rule of cool." In the school of the future, there will be greater specialization at an earlier age, so that students with similar interests and abilities (tribes) will be able to affirm each other and spur each other on to greater accomplishment. In the decentred school of the future, oddness will become normal. There won't be any homecoming queen or king. The social and academic distinctions between top and bottom, centre and periphery, will dissolve. The fringe-dwellers and the cool kids will be indistinguishable.

11

The Truth About Bullying

Bullying Defined

My definition of bullying is simple: the use of fear or intimidation to gain power and control. The fear wielded by bullies takes four main forms, although they all have the common denominator of shame: physical harm, emotional harm, social exclusion, and public humiliation. We fear all of these things deeply. We have all felt physical pain and emotional pain, and we have all felt left out and embarrassed, but shame goes deeper. Shame has to do with our sense of our own value, both in our own eyes and the eyes of the group. To feel shamed is to feel exposed. We feel vulnerable and weak. We feel as though all our self-doubts and insecurities have been proven right. We really are worthless. We really are pathetic. When we are shamed, the persona drops, and all those dark ghosts that huddle in our psychic closet come screaming out. It is an experience we will do anything to avoid, which sometimes means shaming, degrading, and humiliating others before they have a chance to do it to us — the preemptive strike. This is the emotional economy of the bully. He has been shamed. He has a strong sense of his own inadequacy. It has been exposed in the past, and he has learned what a powerful weapon it can be to lift that veil from another person.

Bullies often learn their trade from their parents, but they can also learn it in the early years of school where many situations can be shaming — wetting one's pants, not being able to answer a simple question correctly ... the list of possible humiliating situations in school is endless.

How they are dealt with in those earliest years can make all the difference in the trajectory of a child's life. Children take their cue from us. The child with undeveloped bladder control is not responsible for his accident, the child who can't get the order of the days of the week right or has trouble remembering which side of the stick to put the ball on for a lowercase B or D is not stupid or lazy. School can become the place where so many of our negative feelings about ourselves take root. At school we learn what it means to pass and fail. For children, life is not such a double-edged sword. When my son Thomas was six and my daughter Rachel five, they completed a swimming course, and on the last day received a certificate. Thomas announced with glee, "Rachel, we passed!" Rachel looked at him quizzically and responded, "Passed what?" For Rachel, it had always been about the fun of swimming, seeing other kids, doing something special with her brother, and the paper only had value because it had a coloured sticker on it. As soon as a child learns the abstraction of passing, they quickly learn its opposite: failing. Bullies are kids who've had more than their share of failure, who do not feel very good about themselves, and seek to feed their self-esteem by taking it away from others.

The first half of my definition, "the use of fear and intimidation," deals with the methods the bully uses. The second half, "to gain power and control," deals with the goals he is trying to achieve. He wants to feel better about himself. He is full of fear and anger. Fear of having his own weaknesses exposed and anger about all the times they have been exposed. Power and control are very positive things. We all want them, and we all need them.

Power is associated with ability. "I can do this." It also has to do with freedom and choice. "I can decide what to do. I have a will." For many bullies, this will to power has been thwarted repeatedly. They feel very powerless. Either someone has robbed them of their power by trying to control them or they have felt the powerlessness of not being able to do something that others are able to do — perhaps something as simple as tying one's shoes in grade one.

Control is another positive thing. Control has to do with our relationship to the external world, to be able to manage one's environment. When a child grows up with little feeling of control over his external world, he may seek to control others. When children are raised with a healthy sense of power and control over their own lives, they grow up to be confident, secure, self-directing adults who feel no need to rob others of their power and control. When a child is denied positive experiences of power and control from a very early age, this deficit will lead to the compensatory behaviour we call bullying.

I worked for one administrator who had been raised by an overbearing, domineering father who allowed his son very little leeway. As a boy, he had little power or control over his own life or his environment. When he got into a position of power himself, first the classroom, and later the main office, he demonstrated all the characteristics of a bully. I always used to feel that this man brought his father to work with him every day. It was almost as though he was showing his father what a "big man" he was now. He was making up for all those years of powerlessness and lack of control.

When we know that bullies are seeking power and control in negative ways, a simple solution is to offer them positive ways of achieving the same goal. Bullies should be put in situations where they can experience success. Success is synonymous with personal power and a feeling of control over oneself and one's environment. This is achieved through freedom of choice. The specific ways in which this can be done will vary widely. I think of the brilliant honour-roll girl who was a terrible bully to many of her peers. She felt incredible insecurity about her intellectual giftedness. Her hovering parents treated her as a trophy child, and she lived in constant fear of losing their conditional love by falling below the high standard that had become her normal. She would have benefited greatly from an honest discussion of her fears with other gifted students who felt the same pressures or who had a healthier sense of their own value and could show her what that was like. I think of the overweight boy in grade nine who had been teased from his youngest days and now made it his project to bring others down too. He could be taken and guided through a positive weight-loss and exercise program. I have worked with students who, after losing two or three pounds, see a possible positive trajectory where they are in control. I have seen students who struggle academically matched up with younger students, "reading buddies," and make huge gains in their self-esteem as a result. When we punish, humiliate, and degrade the bully we only make the problem worse. As A.S. Neill said, "Hate breeds hate, and love breeds love." Bullies need our love.

Humans are Pack Animals

A fundamental fact that helped me understand bullying better was the simple insight that humans are pack animals. We are a social species. We have always organized ourselves in groups: families, clans, tribes, later on in feudal groupings, and eventually nation states. We need to belong to something larger than ourselves. Patriotism and nationalism attest to this fact. The positive aspect of this is that groups provide us with two very important things: protection and a sense of identity. We seem to naturally organize ourselves into groups that can be based on any criteria that helps define us: religious affiliation, hobbies, age group, music, video games — the list is endless.

The second thing about packs is the fact that all packs have pecking orders. Every pack has its dominant figure that we honour with the positive term "leader." The leader may be a positive or negative figure, but the fact remains that he has found his way to the top of the pecking order through various means — democracy, popularity, force.

When we have a naturally occurring pack like a church group, a political party, or a heavy metal fan club, the pecking order has its own internal logic. When one joins the pack, one buys into that logic and it is relatively uncontested. Natural pecking orders seem to arise organically in those groups that we choose and the criteria for dominance bear some correlation to the values the group holds.

But what about when we find ourselves in packs we did not choose or which are artificially constructed — like school. Twenty-five or thirty ten-year-olds would not naturally band together as a group in order to learn. So what happens when we create these artificial groupings? It is inevitable that a pecking order will have to be established, because that is our nature, but according to what criteria will dominance be determined? In a perfect world, we might imagine that the smartest child would rise to the top and all the others would try to emulate him or her. Or the kindest child would rise to the top and the other children would take him or her as their role model. In the artificial world of school, something more primitive happens.

When we group children according to age only, they find other ways of organizing themselves into a hierarchy, and the one they eventually settle on is conformity to social norms. Dominance is achieved by being the most conformed and the pecking order is determined by adherence to these dictates. Sometimes the standard of conformity is dictated by the broader consumer culture, other times kids can create subcultures that have their own rules. Gangs are a highly visible example of this, but the clique of grade eight girls can be just as strict about what's acceptable and what's not. What makes this so tragic is the way the incredible diversity among children quickly becomes a liability. As each year passes, the child learns that sticking out is the worst possible thing and fitting in is best. We have a word for this fitting in. It's called being cool, and so much individuality is lost as a result. Bullying becomes the dominant mode of natural selection in this man-made jungle. We take a tribe-loving species, we superimpose upon it an artificial homogenizing institution, and the results can be crazy-making.

Who Are the Bullies?

The discussion about bullying needs to be broadened to include a consideration of all forms of bullying. When we isolate the bullying issue to the school yard, we ignore a cultural milieu in which bullying is quite common, and we feed into the general acceptance of this way of dealing with each other. When we, as a culture, hyper-focus on one thing, it is often an indication that we do not want to look at other things. Bullies can be:

- Students
- Siblings
- Parents
- Teachers
- Administrators
- Coaches
- Co-workers
- Neighbours
- Spouses
- Governments
- Media images

Some of the worst bullying cases I have dealt with have been bullying by siblings. Stephen was a sensitive, effeminate kid who loved drama and photography. He went home almost every day to a verbal or physical "beating" by his two brothers — both "jock" hockey players. I have had colleagues ask me to sit with them on parents' night because they feared the bullying parent they knew was coming. There are some parents I will not call about their child's performance or behaviour at school because I worry about the methods the parent will use to deal with it. I have spoken to elementary school classes about bullying, where I was ushered into the room and had to wait while the teacher, in a loud threatening voice, "read the riot act" to the class: that no one was to make a sound during my presentation or they would have that teacher to deal with afterwards. I could see that this was a classroom, like too many classrooms, run on fear. I have worked for a number of principals who I would easily call bullies. They were not equipped for the role of leader. The only tool they had was a hammer, so everything appeared to them as a nail. Coaching is another situation where the "tough guy" persona is valued — sometimes to the extreme. I have known too many parents who gave up coaching organized sports themselves or pulled their children out because of the bullying atmosphere. One teacher came up to me after a bullying pres- entation and told me how the biggest bully in her life was the custodian at her school. Another teacher told how she had to go on stress leave because of the bullying she endured from the head secretary. It is not always bosses who are the bullies, although they are in an ideal position to do so. Sometimes it is co-workers, and the workplace becomes like an unsupervised school yard. Neighbours can bully each other over leaves falling on each other's lawns or dogs peeing on each other's grass. When husbands and wives bully each other in subtle ways, it has a slow, corro- sive effect on the couple, their marriage, and the children. When they do it in more dramatic ways, we call this domestic violence.

Two of the biggest bullies in the playground are governments and media images. Government is based on an adversarial model, positively referred to as checks and balances, but negatively lived out as winners and losers, those who are right and those who are wrong. The goal is not to arrive at the best policies for a country, the goal is to have your party's pos- ition win and the other party's position lose. To win at all costs. This goal is often achieved through the use of fear and intimidation as well as public ridicule and humiliation. We see the most childish, rude, and hurtful comments thrown freely around in our parliaments and legislatures. We see even worse character assassination and mud-slinging in the attack ads that pass for political advertising. Statements are made and things are done that would easily get a child sent to the principal's office were he to say or do similar things at school. The language used in attack ads is no different from the language used in cyber-bullying. Bullying is also found on the international stage where the country with the biggest stick (weapons and money) calls the shots. In politics, might makes right. Retaliation is a virtue.

The use of fear and intimidation lies behind almost all commercial advertising. The unspoken moral of every commercial is if you buy this, you will be cool and accepted and therefore happy. If you don't buy this, you will be vulnerable to the negative judgements of others. Apple took this to the most literal level in their long-running ad campaign that showed two men standing side-by-side. The one who owned the Apple product was young, hip, and confident. The one who owned the PC was middle-aged, awkward, and insecure. The choice was clear. While the tone of the commercial was tongue-in-cheek, the underlying strategy was bullying: the use of fear and intimidation (You won't be cool) to gain power and control (market share).

The Time I was Bullied

My first experience of bullying dates back to around grade three or four. I don't remember the circumstances. I just remember that some older boy planned to beat me up on my way home from school. Was it something I said or did? I can't remember. I just remember the fear. How could I get home and avoid him on the main road we all walked, which was out of sight of the school and my house. The strategy I chose was avoidance. For the first couple of days, I would run from school as soon as the bell rang. I was way ahead of the crowd, and it worked, but was not sustainable. I finally shared my problem with my mother, and told her my next strategy was going to be taking the long way around the block. This would add about ten minutes to my five-minute walk home. I don't remember what other advice Mom gave me, but she dismissed the idea of going the other way as silly. I remember feeling very alone with my problem and very scared. Within a few days, it happened. I was walking on Paisley Road, my usual route, with the regular crowd of kids coming home from school, when he jumped on me and started punching me. I was on the ground, and I didn't fight back much, so it wasn't much of a fight for him. The thing that I will always remember is that while I was lying there being punched, an adult man, perhaps in his thirties, walked by. I looked at him imploringly, feeling he was my only hope. Surely he would do something. This situation was so blatantly unjust. He averted his eyes and walked around the group of kids that had formed to watch the fight. I will never forget that.

This story raises two topics: the strategies kids use to deal with bullying, and the role of adults in the problem. In all the literature on bullying, there are three main strategies that emerge:

1. Avoidance.
2. Talking back.
3. Telling an adult.

AVOIDANCE

Some people would call avoidance running away from your problem, and they would say this is a bad thing to do, that we need to face our problems and deal with them. This is true when the problem is unavoidable, but sometimes a problem *can* be gotten rid of by avoiding it, especially when the problem exists outside of us or outside of our immediate sphere. If a child is put in a class with a bully who has targeted him in the past, those kids should be put in separate classes. The same goes for organized sports teams. Do not go to the part of the playground where the bully goes. Do not sit in the section of the bus the bully sits in. When you avoid the bully, you are not running away from the problem, you are dealing with the problem. The question becomes how high a price the victim should have to pay for the actions of the bully. If the avoidance strategies are easy to implement and get results, fine. If the child is bending over backwards to avoid the bully, or the strategy simply isn't practical because the victim and the bully are always in close proximity, then it is time to move on to the next two steps.

TALKING BACK

If avoidance does not work or is not possible, then the child should turn and face the bully. This is harder for some children than others. I have found that sometimes nice, polite, well-behaved children are bullied precisely because they are always so nice and polite. They can be quite passive. The bully senses this vulnerability. The polite, quiet child is not good at talking back or advocating for himself. He readily accepts external controls. When the bully moves in, he doesn't have the experience of pushing back against things he feels are unreasonable or uncomfortable. He has always just accepted whatever is done to him.

This is a hard topic because it appears to blame the victim for being bullied. I am simply talking about the psychological profile I have seen in many bullied kids over the years. It could be argued that the parent is the child's first bully. If we look again at my definition of bullying, the use of fear and intimidation to gain power and control, we can see that parenting, by its very nature, is a power relationship and has parallels with the bullying situation. If you don't behave at the dinner table, I'll send you to your room. You cannot go to the mall with your friends because you're too young. While these are reasonable well-intentioned statements, to the child they can be felt as arbitrary and unjust. In a home with healthy communication, children are free to talk back. The talking back should be, in fact it usually *will* be, done in the same tone the parents use. If a parent speaks reasonably and honestly, a child will learn to speak reasonably and honestly, and they will be better able to talk back to other voices they find unreasonable or unjust, like the taunting of a bully. If the child is spoken to in a "my way or the highway" tone, they will learn one of two things: passivity in the face of negative power (being bullied) or they will deal with their feelings of impotence by copying the negative power of the adult and look for weaker subjects who they can boss around as they were bossed around. They will become bullies.

Talking back includes body language, an area where some kids need coaching. They need to be shown how to hold their head up, how to make eye contact if the situation demands it, and how to speak in a firm, clear voice. For the introverted child, this can be very difficult. It does not feel natural for them. It might need to be taught as a conscious persona to adopt in particular situations. Many introverts learn, consciously or unconsciously, to adopt the kinds of behaviours required in particular situations like the board room or the dinner party. For the introverted child, the playground or the back of the bus may be the first place they learn to play a role for the sake of social survival. In a perfect world, the quiet, polite child would spend his or her day with other quiet, polite children. But at a very young age our children find themselves in social settings where they are exposed to a huge range of behaviours — some radically different from those they experienced at home. Again, we are left with the question of how much of the bullying problem can be traced back to the very existence of age-specific groups spending long periods of time in confined spaces.

TELLING AN ADULT

The third strategy, after avoidance and talking back, is reporting to an adult. Once again we are back to the issue of children having adults in their lives who they feel they can trust and talk to honestly — in short, adults with whom they have meaningful and positive relationships. If these exist, then the child will naturally talk about any problems he or she is having. Difficulties are part of the fabric of life, and children should feel free to talk about their bad experiences as well as their good ones. From an early age, we need to show that we are available and open.

Why Kids Don't Report Bullying

Many young people have told me the reason they don't tell their parents about their problems is they don't want their parents to "freak out." Very often our emotional response just becomes an added burden for the child. They are dealing with their own feelings about the problem, and then they have to deal with the parent's feelings as well. Many kids will choose to handle their problems alone simply because it gives them a feeling of greater control. One of the reasons parents freak out when they hear about bad things happening to their children is they feel a loss of control. There is a part of us that would like to have total control over our children's lives, so that we could prevent anything bad ever happening to them. When we hear of something negative in their lives, it reminds us that we do not have control. We feel anger at those who have hurt our child, those who are not helping the child, and the whole situation that gave rise to the negative experience. If there is one emotion that children are extremely sensitive to in their primary attachment figures it is anger. If they say something, and Mom and Dad get angry, then they are the cause of their anger. "Mom's mad. I'm bad." This is a spontaneous formulation in many kids' minds. In addition, the child feels a sense of danger. They feel the next possible step could be punishment or rejection. Even though our anger is not directed at the child, it fills the room, and the child can be overwhelmed by it. It just takes one or two of these kinds of episodes for the child to learn not to say anything that will make Mom or Dad angry or upset.

As parents, we need to be in control of our feelings. This is not to say we need to deny or repress our feelings, but we need to be sensitive to their power in a child's emotional life. We can talk to our spouse, adult friends, or other family members about how we feel. To the child, we can freely express our feelings of sympathy, concern, and comfort, but we must model for the child a calm, rational approach. Children need to read from our emotional response that their own thoughts and feelings are valid and their problem is solvable. A child feeling confused and victimized does not need the added confusion or the vulnerable feeling caused by a parent who has "lost it."

Kids are also afraid of being re-victimized by becoming the scandal-of-the-week. They do not want attention drawn to themselves. They want the situation to be dealt with as discretely as possible. They already feel vulnerable and exposed for having been centered out by the bully, and the thought of having that feeling amplified by adult involvement is just too much to bear. For this reason, it is very important to include the bullied child in the response to be taken. We need to explain to the victim what the various options are and ask the child for their input. As a teacher, I might say, "Would you like me to speak to the bully?" "Is it okay if I tell the bully you talked to me?" "What, exactly, do you want the bully to stop doing?" As a parent, I might say, "Is it okay if I talk to your teacher?" "These are the possible things that the teacher could do. Which of those do you think would be best?" This, of course, is just a first step. The follow up stages are just as important. I have often seen adults take one step and then feel they had dealt with the problem.

In most of the cases I have dealt with, the child has agreed to my talking to the bully. I tell the victim it will be a very discrete conversation, and that there is a pretty good chance the bullying will stop. A typical conversation with the bully goes like this:

> Josh told me that you call him names when he gets on the bus in the morning. Josh doesn't like this, and I told him I would talk to you. You're not going to say anything to Josh when he gets on the bus tomorrow morning. I'm going to speak to Josh tomorrow and ask him if you called him names, and I expect he'll say no. If anyone was bothering you, I would do the same for you.

A couple of notes about this conversation:

1. Notice that it is pretty one-sided. If the bully begins a defence, of course we can listen to it, but it would be counter-productive to get into a court case of all the evidence at this early stage of intervention when we are simply trying to stop a specific behaviour. If things escalated, then more details could be brought in. In my experience, if the bully is spoken to respectfully and factually there is little push-back.

2. The conversation with the bully has to happen with a tone of complete respect and factual detail. The only emotion that should be perceptible is determination on the part of the adult to see this issue resolved, to see this behaviour come to an end. I have found over the years that speaking to children in a respectful tone is one of the most difficult things to describe or explain. There are adults who can do it, and there are others who, no matter how hard they try, their tone sounds condescending or accusatory.

3. The behaviour is described in very specific and measurable terms: what, where, when — calling names, on the bus, in the morning. There may be other behaviours, but often it is best to focus on something very specific just to break the cycle of verbal humiliation.

4. Use as few words as possible.

5. Use simple, concrete language.

6. "I told him I would talk to you" and "I would do the same for you" are very powerful messages that there are adults around who are not just playing the role of policemen lying in wait to catch kids being bad. There are adults around who are genuinely concerned and will stand up for kids when they are being victimized. In many schools, there is a kind of "us and them" relationship between kids and adults. Bullies especially feel this way because of all the times they've gotten in trouble. Kids need to know there are adults who really are on their side — even the side of the bully.

7. The most important part of this conversation is the mention of follow up, that I am going to check with Josh to hear how things went. And the positive surprise add-on will be that when I find out Josh was not bullied the next morning on the bus, I will take the time to find the bully, let's call him Jeremy, and tell him that I was very glad to hear that nothing was said and that I'm going to keep checking with Josh now and then. And then one might just say to Jeremy, "If anyone ever bothers you, you let me know."

8. In the context of a case study, the author can easily create a happy ending to show the effectiveness of his strategy. What if the behaviour does not stop? What if the behaviour escalates? What if the bully is angered and retaliates? In this case, the process is simply repeated with the same firmness of purpose and the same follow up. But because we started the process at a low level, we can now slowly escalate the consequences. This is an important point, because adults need to have a next hand to play if things do not go as planned. Sometimes we escalate to all-out war before any backroom diplomacy has gone on. The key benefit in backroom diplomacy is that it allows both parties to save face. As soon as things escalate, you have created a situation where there will be a winner and a loser, and, sadly, sometimes the bullied child can end up being the loser. So, when the behaviour does not stop, the next conversation might go something like this:

"I spoke to Josh, and he said you did it again this morning. Now, you've got to understand that this can all end right here with me talking to you about it, or we can go to the principal and that will involve detentions and suspensions and we can even go up from there. It's your choice. You're either going to stop picking on Josh, or this will get worse."

What Can Parents Do?

The scenarios described above involve teachers and administrators who are on the front lines with our kids every day. They have the advantage of being able to talk to the bully. This is a fundamental point, and teachers and administrators need to realize this key advantage they have, and they need to use it. The hardest part for a parent can be the feeling of powerlessness because they can only speak to their child and adults who have the power to do something about the problem. This is why it is so important that teachers and administrators take bullying seriously, if only out of respect and sympathy for the worried parent.

Parents must persevere in their attempts to have the problem dealt with, but, again, they must not "freak out." Parents need to interact with the school in as rational a way as possible. The facts are the facts. Do not let your emotions cloud them, or you run the risk of stirring up the emotions of the teachers and administrators you rely on. This may not seem fair, but it is the way the system "works." Almost all educational jurisdictions have objective policies and procedures for how bullying is to be dealt with, but we know from experience that these policies and procedures are still very susceptible to human interpretation and human willingness to follow through. Parents should know what these policies are and must persevere to ensure that they are enforced.

Should I Speak to the Parent of the Bully?

This question exposes one of the most challenging problems in dealing with parents. There is such a broad spectrum of personalities, attitudes, and parenting styles. These differences can become even more pronounced when we add the emotional element of talking about the behaviour of another person's child. We can all be very polite and civilized when there is nothing at stake, but when our behaviour or the behaviour of our child is called into question, our defences immediately go up, and this does not bode well for a healthy conversation.

I have seen parents approach other parents where both had the attitude that it takes a village to raise a child, we're all in this together, let's talk, let's work this out, we all want what's best for the kids, and progress is made. On the other hand, I have seen the attack and defend stances taken, and the problem escalates far beyond what it originally was. The parents of bullies often have a psychological profile similar to that of their bullying child. There is an essential insecurity. Defend-and-attack is the default mode when there is any feeling of threat. They feel a lot of conflict around issues involving authority, power, and control. This is why principals will usually advise parents of bullied kids not to approach the bully's parents. It is important to be aware of these two possible scenarios when deciding whether or not to talk to the parent of a bully.

Mediation

Mediation can be a valuable strategy because the mediator becomes the neutral focus of the discussion. Comments are directed to him or her. One party can hear what the other party has to say, but they are not the direct recipients. The attack and defend stance may still be there, but it is mediated through a third person and thus the negative energy can be reduced. Ideally, the mediator would be an adult who has no connection with the power structure of the school. This is not always practical, so the teacher or principal ends up playing this role. In some schools, older students have been trained as mediators, an excellent option for keeping things on a human level rather than an institutional power structure level.

The mediator should speak to each child separately first to achieve clarity about the facts. Feelings must be acknowledged and discharged before they can be separated from the facts. If parents are involved, even greater care must be taken. There can be a lot of anger and fear in the conversation, core issues that most people have not dealt with very much, so years of pent up emotion get released. When the veneer is cracked, the fallout can be huge. Once the emotional temperature of the situation is lowered, there can be a much more productive conversation.

The Key Role of the Adult

The only guarantee against bullying is the presence of a strong adult. Let's go back to that scene of me lying on the sidewalk at the age of ten being beaten up by an older boy. That man who walked by had to change his path in order to get around us. There are many adults who change their path in order to avoid what is uncomfortable, what is happening right in front of them. There are many reasons why they do this. Sometimes they honestly believe they are doing the right thing. They think that bullying is just part of life and you have to tough it out, that it will make you stronger, that the bullied kid somehow deserves it or was asking for it. Other adults might say to themselves it is none of their business. It's between the kids. There is no reason for them to get involved.

The bottom line is that kids need adults. They need strong adults who are willing to step up and play the role of an adult in their lives. I see so many adults who are simply not willing or not able to take on the role that kids need them to play. In the bullying situation a very primitive imperative has taken over — the desire to gain dominance through the humiliation or submission of another. If we do not believe in social Darwinism — the notion that some people are innately superior to others and deserve to be dominant — if we believe that all people have equal value and deserve equal respect, then we are compelled to step in when we see someone being degraded or abused.

What Is a Strong Adult?

Sometimes the bullying situation is solved by the intervention of an adult who is simply an even bigger bully. One or both of the kids are punished or humiliated in order to stop the behaviour. In this case the bullying adult is only contributing to the problem, making the bully even angrier and re-victimizing the victim. Kids need adults who are not bullies. In institutional settings, bullying is often dealt with according to policies and procedures — sometimes a "zero tolerance" policy in which there is no room for discussion or nuance. The adult in the situation is bound by the policies and procedures and simply becomes the administrator of a prescribed response listed in a binder somewhere. As Barbara Coloroso has said, "Zero tolerance means zero thinking." Every bullying situation is unique, and both kids would be much better served if there was some attempt to understand the inner dynamic that brought both the bully and the victim to this point. This takes time and effort as well as compassion for both kids.

The strong adult is a person who has done some inner work and transcended the role of teacher, principal, or parent. Their values do not come from a binder of standard procedures nor the collective values of the culture. They operate according to a set of self-chosen principles that they are able to apply in various situations. They have taken ownership of their authority and use it for the service of others, not to have power and control over others. They have given some thought to the issue of bullying and arrived at a humane and enlightened approach to dealing with it.

Law Has Replaced Morality

The rise in bullying is a by-product of the weakening of a civil society. In a culture where the threshold of what is considered rude or mean has moved drastically, kids have a very broad sense of what can be said and done with impunity. We live in an age dominated by postmodern thought that sees all truth statements as biased. Postmodernism does not accept the possibility of objective truth and morality. These things are socially constructed. While the postmodern critique has done a valuable job of challenging dominant vested interests, it has left us with a culture where anything can be said and all points of view are equally valid. Postmodernism rightly challenged biases like racism and sexism. Civil rights and greater equality for women are the tangible fruits of these efforts. But postmodernism seems to have thrown out the baby of morality with the bathwater of abuse of power. Any talk of morality is associated with organized religion — institutions notorious for their abuses of power. It sounds old-fashioned or conservative to talk about morality today, as though one wants to take us all back to the old days when men were men and women were women.

Can we still talk about morality? We need moral codes that are deeper than laws. We need guidelines for living and boundaries for our behaviour that are not just made out of rules. The only real guidelines many kids have today are laws. You can do or say whatever you want as long as it isn't illegal. The criminal code has become a moral code. Calling somebody fat or stupid or making fun of something they said or did, whether in the classroom or on social media, is not illegal, and for many kids, that makes it okay. Our notions of common decency are no longer held in common. I counselled a teenager whose parents caught him sending pictures of himself naked to someone who had lured him on the Internet. The police were involved, and, while no charges were laid against the boy, he was told that it was illegal, that it could be considered trafficking in child pornography. I asked him, "If if wasn't illegal, would you still do it?" He was completely unable to answer this question. He looked at me with utter confusion and said, "I don't know." This is the situation our young people face today — a world that allows unprecedented kinds of behaviours but has nothing to say about the morality of those behaviours. Young people have no yardsticks by which to measure things, no moral codes to apply to unfamiliar situations. The adults in their lives seem just as confused. This is why our society needs good, strong, wise adults more than ever.

This issue is particularly relevant to teachers who have traditionally been seen as that good, strong, wise adult. This is becoming harder as each year passes. Most people spend their day working and living with people who are pretty similar. If you are dealing with the general public behind a counter, on the phone, or in a service capacity, the interactions are usually brief, one-to-one, and certain social codes are observed. In elementary school a teacher is interacting with children who have not fully adopted a common core set of adult behaviours. By high school, they have adopted the codes of a culture that has very broad boundaries determining what's acceptable and what's not. A teacher also stands in front of dozens of different homelives and parental influences. The child from a strict religious home where swearing would never be tolerated sits beside a student who learned the most colourful words at her mother's knee. I only use swearing as a simple example of the shift in boundaries that has occurred.

A more disturbing example would be to quote some of the racist and sexist comments that a teacher can hear in any classroom — spoken aloud in a class discussion, spoken quietly in individual conversations, or just assumed in particular contexts. One student, writing on the topic of "The perfect girlfriend" wrote, "She needs to be able to take a few slaps." The idea itself is appalling, but what is just as disturbing is the fact that he felt he had the license to write this. Does he live in a world where this attitude is acceptable? Is it his version of common decency? He shows no awareness of external norms, except as prescribed by law, and even that code has failed as he thinks "a few slaps" lie outside the law. Because we deal intimately with so many children, teachers see the fragmented nature of our culture's moral landscape. It can be very difficult for a teacher who would like to assume some kind of common moral ground or teach a common moral ground.

12

The Curriculum Debate

WHAT DO KIDS *NEED* TO LEARN?

Why Should I do This? I'm Never Going to Use It!

One of the most challenging questions schools have had to deal with ever since we decided to send everyone is what should be taught? What is relevant? What is useful? What are the skills and knowledge we want *all* citizens to have? This wasn't as hard a question when school only went up to grade eight, but when we decided to keep everyone in until the age of seventeen or eighteen, this became a much more complicated question. Before mass schooling, elementary school was a place to learn basic literacy and numeracy. A prescribed basic curriculum was a logical thing for students who would eventually go back to the farm, out to work, or get married and start a life of their own at a relatively young age. Before the Second World War, secondary school was only attended by a small group who showed a particular aptitude for academics generally. Requiring all of them to study math, sciences, and liberal arts was seen as reasonable. These were kids who, for the most part, could handle a rigorous, broad curriculum.

After the war, when large factory schools became the norm due to the baby boom, we had to think up new approaches for this much more diverse group. The range of course choices was broadened, and in traditional subject areas that we felt every student needed, like math, science, and English, students were streamed by ability. The list of mandatory courses remained relatively unchanged. As we move into the future, an essential standard core curriculum becomes harder to define. The last strong voice in this area was E. D. Hirsch who called for "cultural literacy" in the form of a core body of knowledge that every student should know. In the 1990s he spawned an industry with his Core Knowledge Series of books, which included *What Your Preschooler Needs to Know* all the way through to *What Your Eighth Grader Needs to Know*. These books included actual detailed lists of what he considered to be essential core knowledge. He wanted to make this knowledge available to every public school child regardless of gender, race, or income level. It was a noble effort founded on noble principles, but represents a last gasp for the factory school before the Internet went public around 1993. Ironically, his vision is mostly carried on today in elite private schools that still adhere to the "great works" model. In this new decentered world of instant access to an almost infinite amount of information (both visual and print), the entire concept of a core curriculum relevant to every child has been swept away.

School as Social Programming

Since we had the whole youth population as a captive audience for approximately twelve to fourteen years, this was seen as an excellent opportunity for social programming. We could teach those courses and topics we felt were necessary for success, and, perhaps more importantly, those values and behaviours that we felt every citizen should possess. As time went on, more and more items were added to this social agenda. School became the place where any social problem could be dealt with through the delivery of a lesson, unit, or course. The school system became a kind of intravenous tube through which we could administer all kinds of remedies for our social ills. Road safety, littering, racism, sexism, childhood obesity, teen pregnancy, addiction, cancer, community service, citizenship, patriotism, and world peace could all be dealt with in the classroom. As a result of all these "add ons" the curriculum in schools became very fragmented and confused. Literacy activities nudged out literature study, citizenship units nudged out the study of history, and making posters and pamphlets for various causes became the content of art classes.

The problem with this social programming paradigm is that it has a way of killing learning. As soon as we turn something important or interesting into curriculum, it becomes watered down, packaged, and sequenced.

In short, boring. Mandatory civics courses are one example. In theory, they are a very good idea — teach kids about their place in a democracy and how the democratic system works. In practice, the course becomes much less than that. Students are often taught by teachers who have little interest because it is not their area of specialty, but most of all, the students realize this is a stand-alone course or unit with a political agenda. The mandatory nature of the course makes it smack of propaganda and manipulation. Kids end up being turned off politics. The students can sense that this is one of those "because it's good for you" things, and teenagers in particular don't deal well with being told what's good for them.

The most troubling example of this backfiring effect is anti-drug programs. When teens and pre-teens are told what *not* to do, we are simply telling them what's cool. If adults don't want you to do something, it must be good — or at least worth trying. Adolescents have two main goals: to define themselves as different from their parents and to fit in with their peer group. When talk turns to the pervasive use of drugs among teens, this is like an instruction video on how to be a rebel.

Another example of social programming backfiring is the mandatory study of French in most Canadian schools. The acquisition of a second language is one of the most positive things a person could pursue. How can something so positive become so negative? Because it is forced. All learning should happen on the principle of attraction, not compulsion. Those who want to learn French will learn it. Those who don't want to and are forced will resist learning it and grow to hate it. How many students actually hate French and resent Quebec because of this politically motivated social programming strategy?

In the school system of the future there will be much greater freedom of choice. Students who have been raised in this system of choice-responsibility will choose the courses they know they need and in which they are interested. School will be a much pleasanter place.

One Diploma Does Not Fit All

We live according to the myth that a high school diploma means one thing, that teenagers who have high school diplomas have a common set of skills and knowledge. This is not the case. As our student population has become more and more diverse, the school system, out of necessity, has been morphing into a broad range of delivery methods, content, and standards of achievement. This process that has been going on, officially and unofficially, for years, needs to be acknowledged more formally. In the later decades of the twentieth century, as the baby boom passed through the system and went on to university in large numbers, high school came to be seen as the preparation ground for university. It was seen as part of a continuum with university as the apotheosis. This phenomenon was driven in North America by two forces — the baby boomers with their positive sense of entitlement and human potential and by the immigrant ethos that your children are going to have a better life than you did. More kids than ever before are getting high school diplomas. Has the "meaning" of those diplomas remained consistent over the past fifty years? More students than ever before are attending university and getting degrees. Has the "meaning" of a degree changed?

Is Education Getting Watered Down?

Enrolment in apprenticeship programs has increased significantly over the past twenty years, but the rate of completion has remained constant. As Statistics Canada researchers put it, "the rate of increase for registrations was more than double the rate for completions." When one is learning a trade, we can imagine that there is a certain set of skills and a certain level of ability that has to be explicitly demonstrated. There is no room for subjective evaluation; one cannot dumb down plumbing or electrical work. The pipe must not leak. The lights must go on. In the liberal arts and humanities, standards are much harder to define and therefore are more susceptible to subjective variation. I would guess that the greatest increase in post-secondary enrolment has occurred in arts faculties. In the sciences and the professional faculties, again, standards are easier to uphold. The answer is right or wrong. High school English teachers often envy their math and science colleagues for whom evaluation is a much more objective process.

University Affairs is a publication of the Association of Universities and Colleges of Canada. In a 2011 article entitled "University for the masses may be oversold. Are students somehow getting smarter? I doubt it,"

Christine Overall describes a dilemma that has faced high school teachers for the past few decades and is now being raised at universities.

> We can continue to dumb-down the curriculum to make it more accessible, by lowering the quantity of reading and writing, the difficulty of tests and the sophistication of lectures and assignments. University instructors are thereby co-opted into helping to make university no more advanced than high school.
>
> Or, we can attempt to hold the line, failing more students, dealing with larger numbers of student complaints and crises, seeing students avoid our courses if they possibly can and facing potential administrative reprisals (the hazard is greater for the non-tenured). That choice incurs career risks as well as personal and professional misery for faculty members.

In other words, as social promotion has become the norm in high school, will social promotion take over in academia?

The only way to avoid the vacuous option of social promotion — diplomas and degrees that mean nothing — is to create more diversity within the system. If we think of school as an ecosystem, we must remember that nature abhors a monoculture. University should be just one choice among many — all legitimate, dignified, socially acceptable, and economically rewarding.

Christine Overall suggests that universities limit their enrolments to those who are truly capable.

> I'd like to think there is a third possibility. We can try arguing that perhaps not so many students should go to university. We can even challenge the idea that university is job preparation or, worse, mere certification of job readiness. Sometimes it is, but sometimes it isn't. Sometimes a university education is about learning for its own sake, the love of discovery and the challenge of stretching one's mind.

This may be a valid option for universities where the slide is only beginning, but it is not an option for high schools. Our students are required *by law* to be there. This has forced high schools to be much more "creative" in their delivery of curriculum and their evaluation of outcomes. This kind of creativity has varied greatly between jurisdictions. It sounds like a contradiction to say we must begin to formalize the current diversity of forms, but we must surrender the idea of the single educational system with its one diploma. This will be the decentered school. To those who love the one-size-fits-all myth, such a notion sounds like a many-headed hydra, an uncontrollable monster that doesn't know which way it's going or who is in charge. This is why we need to change the metaphor of school from a factory to a garden — not a monoculture but one that embraces and celebrates the biodiversity of children.

Instead of a Standardized Curriculum and One Diploma

Instead of a standardized curriculum, the boundary between school and real life will be blurred. Experience leading to competent performance will be valued as much or even more than courses, credits, and school-issued certificates. Universities, colleges, and high schools have already begun to replace book-learning with more hands-on experience. We have seen the growth of co-op programs where students get academic credit for on-the-job experience. Field placements and internships are replacing classroom lectures. Apprenticeships need to become a standard method of entering the workforce in a wide range of jobs, not just the trades.

Instead of a single diploma, students in the future will work to develop an academic resume in the same way they work to establish an employment resume today. They will accumulate a portfolio of knowledge, skills, and attitudes that can be marketed to employers or academic institutions — which will still exist as an integral part of a complex educational landscape with a whole array of choices.

13

What We Could Learn From Alternative Models

Homeschooling

Homeschoolers are like the Mennonites or Amish of the educational system. They live off the grid. We are fascinated by them but find them slightly odd. Part of us admires their independence while another part of us feels sorry for them. They make us uncomfortable because they have chosen a lifestyle that challenges ours. In a world where everyone is trying so hard to fit in, they represent a blatant disregard for this key goal. The first question every homeschooling parent gets asked is "What about socialization?" This is code for "What about fitting in?" Only later do questions about learning get asked.

The other unsettling response from parents to homeschooling is the idea that they could not bear to spend so much time with their own children! Parents count down the days in late August when they will be able to send their children back to school. Children are seen as an inconvenience, another "thing" to juggle in our busy lives.

When we do finally get to the topic of learning, the information becomes even more challenging to the status quo. Homeschooled children can cover the same curriculum school does in about half to one third the time. These children excel in a wide range of areas, but most importantly are able to pursue their own interests from an early age. Homeschoolers go on to university and college in large numbers. Some universities give preferential acceptance to homeschoolers because they know they will retain them as students. One of the biggest un-talked-about problems for post-secondary schools is retention — keeping students once they've been accepted. So many students from mainstream schools drop out because they have no idea what they are interested in, don't know how to learn, and are not self-directed. Homeschooled kids are more likely to know what they are interested in because from a very early age they have been permitted to pursue those interests. This teaches them how to learn, because they do it on their own, without an authority figure standing over them or, conversely, handing out marks, praise, or gold stars.

Homeschooling also testifies to the shocking fact that we simply don't *need* school in order to learn. In fact, we don't even need teachers. Homeschooling exists across a spectrum. At one end is unschooling, in which students are given complete freedom to follow their own interests in whatever way they choose. Adult intervention only occurs when the child asks for it, from a parent, mentor, or some kind of expert in a particular field. At the other end of the spectrum, homeschooling can resemble the traditional classroom, only set up at home. The parent plays the role of teacher, a prescribed curriculum is followed, and sometimes even tests and exams may be administered. Some homeschoolers will take online courses administered by school boards, colleges, or universities.

Whatever one thinks of homeschooling as an option, it does have some things to teach us about children, schools, teaching, and learning.

1. Children are naturally curious. If left to their own devices, they will follow that natural curiosity to astounding ends.
2. Children are capable of managing themselves. They do not require constant supervision and monitoring.
3. Children are intelligent. We are all familiar with the theory of multiple intelligences. School emphasizes two kinds of intelligence over all others: mathematical and linguistic. The homeschooled child is free to exercise and develop whichever intelligence serves his or her learning best.
4. School is an artificial construct that is not essential to learning. In fact, sometimes it can impede learning.
5. Learning can be fun! When you are doing what you love according to your own schedule and without the fear of evaluation, the possibilities are endless.

6. You don't need to be good at everything. A functional ability in some areas is all that is required.

7. Being with your own kids (or any kids) for long periods of time can be lots of fun.

8. Children like being with adults. Some children prefer adult company.

9. Kids do not have to be grouped according to age. They could just as easily be grouped according to area of interest or level of ability.

10. There is no such thing as a lazy child. Freedom of choice unleashes energy. Compulsion breeds apathy.

Montessori Schools

Maria Montessori (1894–1952) was born in the Victorian era and died in the nuclear age. She opened her Casa dei Bambini in Rome in 1907. Today there are an estimated thirty thousand Montessori schools around the world. I'm not sure what Maria Montessori would think of many of the schools that bear her name today. There has been lots of controversy within the movement about just what the essential elements of Montessori's philosophy and practice include, but there are some fundamental principles that all schools could learn from if our goal is to create more humane environments.

Montessori believed that learning was a natural function of the human being, not something that had to be imposed through external force. It is such a simple idea, but our current school system seems to have lost faith in the natural curiosity of children and how to harness it. With our emphasis on prescribed curriculum, the focus has moved away from the child to the outcomes we wish to achieve. The child becomes an object that is acted upon rather than an agent of their own learning. Montessori also believed in the importance of freedom and choice within the learning environment. She talked about freedom within structure and placed a large emphasis on what she called "the prepared environment." Her schools today sometimes emphasize structure more than freedom and tidiness over child-friendly messiness, but I think that is a by-product of parental expectations. Montessori schools are private schools seeking to attract customers, and like all enlightened approaches, often succumb to the pressure of the consumer for a clean, tidy product that shows well. Montessori schools are often chosen today for their "brand" and the more selective clientele they cater to.

Montessori believed in age-mixing. It is so important for kids moving through the developmental stages to see up close what is next on the continuum, to interact with older and younger students in an intimate way that elicits empathy and nurturing toward those who are younger and challenge to come up to the level of those who are older. Age-mixing also denies the myth that our school system operates under, that all kids of a certain age are basically the same. This is a mechanistic idea that justifies sorting kids by birth date for efficiency's sake. It denies the broad range of abilities, interests, and behaviours that can exist between children of the same age.

Montessori believed in the importance of allowing a child to focus on one activity for as long as he or she is interested. This promotes the child's powers of concentration. In the factory school, bells and adult-imposed schedules determine the length of time to be spent on any given activity. Again, efficiency is the deciding principle.

One of her greatest contributions to education was the idea of the child-friendly environment. She was the first person to shorten the legs on desks and chairs and bring colour and light into the classroom. She introduced multi-sensory education, giving as much importance to the child's body as the child's mind. What would Maria Montessori say about some of our classroom environments and our school yards? How could the idea of the prepared environment be applied to high schools? What would a teenager-friendly environment look like?

When Maria Montessori was asked about her method, she said, "There was no method to be seen, what was seen was a child. A child's soul freed from impediments was seen acting according to its own nature." Montessori had a profound faith in the innate wisdom, goodness, and intelligence of children. We would do well to share her faith.

Waldorf Schools

Rudolf Steiner (1861–1925) opened the first Waldorf School in 1919 in Stuttgart, Germany. Since then this model has spread around the world, and in some European countries Waldorf schools are publicly funded. The most important thing we can learn from this model is the balanced attention paid to artistic, practical, and intellectual pursuits. Children begin with experiential learning, free play, movement, and artistic activities like singing, drawing, and listening to stories. Children are also sensitized to nature and the natural rhythms of the seasons. Children are grouped by age ranges of seven-year intervals, not twelve-month intervals as in the traditional school. Like Montessori, age-mixing acknowledges both the spectrum within age ranges and the unique nature of particular developmental periods. Maria Montessori called these "sensitive periods." For Steiner, each seven-year period involved the development of a particular faculty: the body, the spirit, and the intellect. This development is seen as linear as well as spiralling — the body and the spirit continue to develop along with the intellect and the interplay between the three is never forgotten. The Waldorf model brings us back to the issue of educating the *whole* child — body, mind, and soul — something our scientific, mechanistic approach to education has lost sight of.

Democratic Free Schools

The most liberal form of schooling in the world today is the democratic free school. The pioneer of this approach was A.S. Neill (1883–1973). He founded his famous school, Summerhill, in 1921 in Leiston, Suffolk, England. His thesis was simple: "To make the school fit the child — instead of making the child fit the school." He spoke as a former school teacher who had abandoned the premises of factory schooling. "The function of the child is to live his own life — not the life that his anxious parents think he should live, nor a life according to the educator who thinks he knows what is best. All this interference and guidance on the part of adults only produces a generation of robots." Neill had a profound trust in the essential goodness of children. "My view is that a child is innately wise and realistic. If left to himself without adult suggestion of any kind, he will develop as far as he is capable of developing."

Neill's vision stands in stark contrast to the view of human nature that has been hard-wired into the western mind: the idea that people (particularly children) are essentially bad, stupid, and lazy. They need external coercion in order to accomplish anything. Their only motivations are fear of punishment and hope of reward. It is a very dark and primitive view of humans that can be traced back to early Christian theologians like St. Augustine who developed the doctrine of original sin — the idea that we are all born bad. Christian theology has tended to emphasize human weakness, the perils of temptation, and contempt for the body. The body being a double culprit: the source of both our weakness and the temptations themselves.

The modern story that illustrates this bias best is William Golding's classic work, *Lord of the Flies*. A group of English schoolboys are stranded on a deserted tropical island. They divide into two groups, one lead by Ralph, the other by Jack. Ralph represents order, reason, and civilization, while Jack represents the chaotic, primitive, and evil nature of human beings. The novel ends with Jack and his mob defeating Ralph and taking over the island. The moral of the story seems to be that children are basically evil, and their evil natures will triumph in the absence of civilizing institutions (especially British ones). Golding himself was a teacher at a British private boys' school, one of the most civilizing institutions we know of, at least according to our myths about school. When one looks more closely at the inner workings of British private schools in the nineteenth and early twentieth centuries, one could analyze the novel in a different way. Jack and his ruthless mob were simply imitating the adult behaviour they had seen modelled at school — the use of bullying, physical violence, and coercion through fear. Does this morality tale tell us more about the beastly nature of boys or the school system that turned them into beasts?

Our conceptions of human nature will influence the kinds of institutions and systems we create. We need to look honestly at our deepest assumptions about children. Are they innately bad, stupid, and lazy, or good, intelligent, and motivated to learn? For me, the answer is clear. Working closely with kids for over thirty years has done nothing but confirm my faith in the essential goodness, intelligence, and motivation of children. When they fall down in any of these three areas, it is always due to some external factor, what Maria Montessori called "obstacles." The things adults do to children "for their own good" are often harmful. We do them for *our own* good or for the sake of efficiency or out of sheer ignorance. Neill said the yardstick is happiness. If a child is happy, we know we are doing the right thing. This doesn't mean spoiling the child or indulging the child, but it does mean loving the child. Why do we find this so hard?

At Summerhill there are no marks, and formal lessons are given only for those students who want them. Students are completely free to follow their own inclinations. Some play for years. Proof of the benefit of the approach lies in the kinds of students it produces. Students from democratic free schools go on to all levels of post-secondary education, the professions, and the world of business. They experience great success in the "real world" because they approach it on their own terms, with confidence and determination, qualities innate to a young person who is left to choose his or her own path and take responsibility for that freedom at every step along the way. No child wants to be a failure. When the free child enters the workplace, they quickly see how the game works and will do whatever is required to continue following their chosen path. If it means they have to write an entrance exam, they will prepare for that exam. If it means they have to learn another language, they will learn that language. The free child becomes a self-directed, self-regulating person who choses goals and does what is necessary to achieve them.

We say we are educating children to take their place as citizens in a democracy. Neill took this claim very seriously. Once a week, a "School Meeting" is held at which any issue can be raised for discussion and any question put to a vote. Everyone has one vote — the students and the adults both. If a decision turns out to be a poor one, it can be changed later. Experience is the teacher, not adult fear. Democracy is based on trust. Dictatorships are based on fear. Democracy is messy, but it teaches responsibility. You get what you choose. If you don't like what you've got, choose something else. We are free, and we can create the kind of world we want through the processes and systems we choose. Democratic free schools exist and thrive all over the world. Why is this model not more widely followed?

14

Brave New World

VISIONS OF THE FUTURE

Why Don't Those Inside Change the System?

In his classic study, *Pedagogy of the Oppressed*, Paulo Freire noted how the oppressed internalize the oppressor. The task master or boss becomes a voice in the head, and we obey him even when he's not around. This process happened to most of us in school. We learned to behave out of fear of punishment or hope of reward. We continue to behave even after the possibility of punishment or reward is gone. This phenomenon is particularly common in teachers who, for the most part, come from the ranks of the well-behaved. Teachers are people who did not rock the boat when they were young, were rewarded for it, and entered a profession where boat-rocking is frowned upon. According to Freire, no matter how idealistic the young teacher, the one who sets out "to change the system from within," when that teacher moves up the ladder, he or she comes to imitate the behaviours they once railed against. In other words, institutions reproduce themselves. Change is unlikely to come from those inside.

Children's Liberation

The evidence that schools need to change is found in two places: First, the number of adults who have demonstrably not achieved their full potential, whose lives, in fact, have been limited by the long-term effects of the institution. Secondly, the anger, frustration and boredom felt by so many kids in our schools today, the millions of children being subjected to the same processes that have been in use since the Industrial Revolution.

For millennia, women were not able to realize their full potential because of the restrictions of patriarchy. A similar phenomenon exists among children. They are victims of a system based on power and control, not self-actualization. As women challenged patriarchy in the nineteenth and twentieth centuries, someone needs to challenge the factory school.

The problem is that children are even more powerless than women once were. Where women had to achieve equality with men, children have to achieve equality with adults. We think of children as less than adults. We find the idea of treating children equally difficult because they do not make up a homogeneous group. They are in the process of growing up. The term "child" could be applied to a helpless six-month-old or a six-foot-tall, 180-pound teenager. Where is the dividing line between being a child and being an adult? Various legal thresholds occur at sixteen, eighteen, and nineteen, but the fundamental question remains: when does a child have the right to choose? When is a child free?

We have witnessed so many liberation movements in the twentieth and twenty-first centuries. Is it time for a children's liberation movement? Most liberation movements come about through struggle from the bottom up. Children will only be free when adults relinquish their need for control and listen to what kids are really saying. Children tell us every day how they feel about school through their words, their behaviours and their feelings. A children's liberation movement would be unprecedented because it would require the assistance of the oppressors, something that never happens because the oppressor has so much to lose. The only thing adults have to lose by giving children greater autonomy is our illusion of control and our fear. What children stand to gain is freedom, happiness, and the realization of their full potential.

The Test at the End

1. Is my child happy at school? Why or why not?
2. Was I happy at school? Why or why not?
3. Who invented school? (You do not need to remember dates.)
4. What is the purpose of school?
5. Do schools accomplish the purpose you named in question 4?
6. Could a person learn without school?
   a. If you answered yes, then why do we have schools?
   b. If you answered no, explain why.
7. What were schools like in the past? What are schools like now? What will schools be like in the future? (You can only use creative writing for the third part of the question!)
8. If you could change anything about school, what would you change?
9. If your child could change anything about school, what would he or she change?
10. Whose suggestions in questions 8 and 9 are more valid?

Bonus Questions:
1. What does it mean to be "smart?"
2. What word is the opposite of "smart?" What does that word mean?

Index

Also by Michael Reist

Raising Boys in a New Kind of World
9781459700437
$24.99

From video games to the Internet, technology and popular culture are having a profound effect on today's boys. Boys need guidance more than ever. But how can we help them do better in school? How can we keep the lines of communication open?

Raising Boys in a New Kind of World is a passionate call for greater empathy. The more we know about boys, the more realistic our expectations of them will be. We need to stop seeing normal boy behaviour as a problem and learn to understand a boy's need for movement, his unique learning styles, and his personal methods of communicating.

Michael Reist writes from the front lines. As a classroom teacher for more than 30 years and the father of three boys, he has seen first-hand the effects that changes in modern culture are having on boys. *Raising Boys in a New Kind of World* is an inspiring and entertaining collection of positive, practical advice on many topics, including discipline, homework, video games, and bullying, and provides numerous tips on how to communicate with boys.

Also of Interest

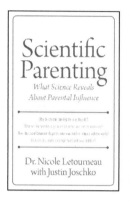

Scientific Parenting
What Science Reveals About Parental Influence
Dr. Nicole Letourneau
9781459710085
$24.99

Combining the expertise of its author — a celebrated expert in parent-infant mental health and mother of two — with the latest findings in gene-by-environment interactions, epigenetics, behavioural science, and attachment theory, *Scientific Parenting* describes how children's genes determine their sensitivity to good or bad parenting, how environmental cues can switch critical genes on or off, and how addictive tendencies and mental health problems can become hardwired into the human brain.

The book traces conditions as diverse as heart disease, obesity, and depression to their origins in early childhood. It brings readers to the frontier of developmental research, unlocking the fascinating scientific discoveries currently hidden away in academic tomes and scholarly journals. Above all, *Scientific Parenting* explains why parenting really matters and how parents' smallest actions can transform their children's lives.

Children Come First
Mediation, Not Litigation When Marriage Ends
Howard H. Irving
9781554887958
$24.99

For three decades Dr. Howard H. Irving has championed the use of divorce mediation outside the adversarial court system to save couples and their children from the bitter legacy of legal wrangling and winner-takes-all custody battles. Now, calling on his vast experience mediating more than 2,000 cases, Irving has written *Children Come First* directly for couples contemplating or undergoing divorce.

In this book the author takes a tripartite approach that points out:

- the dangers of the adversarial approach to divorce,
- the benefits of divorce mediation, and
- how parents can put their children first during and after their divorce.

Children Come First is written in a reader-friendly style with case studies, charts, and diagrams, as well as illustrations from the author's renowned practice. Ultimately, this book takes parents through the process of building a shared parenting plan that places their children's interests uppermost while still addressing the parents' unique situations and needs.

Keep Up If You Can
Confessions of a High School Teacher
Bill Sherk
9781459703575
$24.99

Bill Sherk taught history to Toronto high school students for more than thirty years. With his dynamic, creative, and occasionally unorthodox teaching style, he instilled in his students a passion for history and learning. Sherk was loved by his students and remained in their memories long after graduation.

Keep Up If You Can is a light-hearted and touching memoir that will appeal to anyone who's had a special teacher impact their life.

Fun facts:

- He learned the names of all his students on the first day of school.
- He assigned ancient names to his ancient history students. They called him Sherkules (*SHERK-yoo-leez*).
- After reading *Webster's Dictionary* cover to cover, he encouraged his students to coin new words, and many of these were published in his three dictionaries.
- Firmly believing in physical activity, he would leap atop his desk and lead his students in an aerobic "Sherkout" to a rock-and-roll beat.

Available at your favourite bookseller

 **DUNDURN**

VISIT US AT
Dundurn.com
@dundurnpress
Facebook.com/dundurnpress
Pinterest.com/dundurnpress